Terry Pratchett's
HOGFATHER
The Illustrated Screenplay

Terry Pratchett,
Vadim Jean,
Bill Kaye
&
Stephen Player

ALSO BY TERRY PRATCHETT

Terry Pratchett's

HOGFATHER

The Illustrated Screenplay

Terry Pratchett's Hogfather is a Mob Film Co. (TV) Production for Sky One/ RHI Entertainment

First published in Great Britain in 2006 by
Gollancz
A subsidiary of the Orion Publishing Group
Orion House, 5 Upper St Martin's Lane, London WC2H 9EA

A CIP catalogue record for this book is available
from the British Library

ISBN-13 978 0 57507 929 8
ISBN-10 0 575 07929 0

1 3 5 7 9 10 8 6 4 2

Printed and bound in Italy.

www.orionbooks.co.uk

The Orion Publishing Group's policy is to use papers that are natural,
renewable and recyclable products and made from wood grown in sustainable forests.
The logging and manufacturing processes are expected to conform to the
environmental regulations of the country of origin.

FOREWORD BY TERRY PRATCHETT

Walking around inside my own head

It was the shoes that did it for me. They looked like something Edmund Blackadder had thrown away quite hard. They were right for the period, I was advised, but since the setting was Discworld we had to decide on what period we meant, which we ultimately agreed was Late Georgian without the Late George.

The hat and shirt changed around. My own glasses were swapped for something more antique, but the shoes, by common consent, stayed. And, as I tried them on, I thought, Good grief, this might actually happen! And if they're taking this much trouble over a pair of old shoes, it might actually be done well!

I played the Toymaker, a small but important part that required me to be scared most of the time. Since I spend most of that time face to er . . . face with Death, this was not hard. And, just to ease me gently into my thespianic debut, mine was the first scene on the first day of the shooting of *Hogfather: The Movie*.

And it did happen, and they did take the trouble.

Movies often don't happen. It is their ground state of being. They run the gamut of people with no power to say yes but lots of power to say no, until you believe that movies get made only because people have run out of excuses not to. And then, as one exasperated producer once put it to me, 'When you've convinced all the Treens, they go and change the Mekon.'

But this one got off the ground after quite a pleasant trip down the runway, and, as I saw the development of the script and the storyboards and the sets and the cast list, it began to fly and took me with it. They'd got it, all the way to the top. They knew how it should go, and they were still confident enough to include me in from the script onwards.

We talked about the look of the city of Ankh-Morpork, which had to be 'real' – real bricks, real dirt, real colours. Fantasy isn't the same as weird . . . but London has its secret share of fantasy places, if you have the knowing of such things, and The Mob found them out. It's amazing how ingenuity can do the work of money.

We discussed actors and they got me David Warner as Lord Downey, for example. They also said: 'We've got Michelle Dockery to play Susan. Trust us – she *is* Susan.' And she was. (The other scene on the first day was of Michelle riding the giant hog. During a break, she was kind enough to tell me how well her costume fitted. It's these little details that you cherish . . .)

And I learned the verb 'to snot'. How did I ever manage without it? It's a rather more versatile form of 'to distress', and is the art of making new places and items look as though they are a hundred years old and have been sorely mistreated every day. There's some wonderful snotting in *Hogfather*.

Then they started sending me the rushes, and it was as if all my Hogswatches had come at once.

I talk about it as if it was all for me, but that's how it can feel like, as you walk through the very disorientating tower of the Tooth Fairy or feel the incredibly realistic snow of the Hogfather's Castle of Bones crunch underfoot. Oh, you know, in a vague kind of way, that there are people out there, at the other end of the process, and you also know that even a three-hour movie means that there are good lines and cherished scenes that never even made it as far as the cutting-room floor, but surely the art is to prune or cut away all those pieces that don't fit or aren't needed any more and still leave the soul intact. If you can make an author get the weird sensation that he is walking around the inside of his own head, then you're probably doing it right.

It was fun.

And now it turns out that it wasn't all for me, but for you, too.

Terry Pratchett
Creator

FOREWORD BY VADIM JEAN

Everything starts somewhere. In my case it was Heathrow Airport . . . in the limbo of Departure Lounge Delay without a book. And as I passed the shelf of Pratchetts, stretching off into apparent infinity, something told me that I could resist no longer. Fatefully, from the depths of my memory I recalled a time ten years ago, when my friend Nigel Planer had been forced to postpone his dubbing session for one of my movies as he'd lost his voice after a week of reading unabridged Discworld audio books. If Nigel was prepared to lose his voice for Terry Pratchett, then there had to be something in it.

I didn't stop laughing out loud until, somewhere over Greenland and much to the relief of my fellow passengers, I put *The Colour of Magic* down.

And from the moment Rincewind looked back down over Ankh-Morpork in flames with Twoflower's luggage at his feet and a seven-foot skeleton with the scythe, the robes and the CAPITALISED DIALOGUE had made an appearance, I knew this world had to be in a movie.

Waxing (or as I now realise, Weatherwaxing) lyrical at my desk about my new discovery, I was about to owe a debt of gratitude to James Graham with whom I share an office – for not only does he have a brain the size of a planet, but he's also read every single Discworld novel. Eager to know which book I should read next, he said that now momentous word: *Hogfather*. For your inspiration, James, I shall be forever grateful.

With its sparklingly witty dialogue, fantastic comedic premise (how can Death standing in for Discworld's sort-of Father Christmas not tickle your stocking?), *Hogfather* made me want to read every book in the series. But, most of all, it confirmed what *The Colour of Magic* had started to make me think: that here was what I was born to bring to the screen.

The film industry being what it is, another few years passed before the strange mixture of chance, opportunity, good fortune and timing coincided to make this dream become a possibility. Naturally enough, it started with a meeting about another project entirely. I was supposed to be at their offices in Isleworth for our first meeting with Sky. So, while producers Rod Brown and Ian Sharples were being thoroughly professional, on time and actually there with the Head of Drama, *I* was fifteen miles away in Soho, at entirely the wrong venue. I had never before met the Sky executives, so I must have made a really great first impression – but somehow, on the other end of a mobile phone, and no doubt smoothed by great producing, I did. Most importantly, the Head of Drama said the immortal words: 'What we really want is a sci-fi/fantasy franchise.'

I said the magic words: 'Terry Pratchett'. No one else had yet done it, so my ambition to be the first to bring a live-action adaptation of a Discworld novel to the screen was still possible. You can only dream about the Head of the Channel turning out to be a Pratchett fan – and that was exactly what the visionary James Baker was! The rest, to misquote something somebody somewhere is alleged to have said, will perhaps one day be history.

The combination of a clear idea of how we wanted to treat the book, a trip to Wincanton for Hogswatch, and producer Rod's legendary powers of persuasion helped Terry to recognise that we didn't just want an option on a *property*; we wanted to actually *tell* the story.

So now all that remained was the simple task of adapting the work of a genius . . .

Not having personally written any of the six feature films I've directed meant I was entirely insane – or at least delirious – when I decided that I wanted to do the adaptation myself. Whichever it turned out to be (and you may now, thanks to Gollancz, judge for yourself) the equally barmy producers agreed. They also agreed to the appointment of Phil Parker as script editor. Over the years I've learned more about screenplay writing from Phil than from anyone else, and his contribution to the daunting task of restructuring the interweaving stories and complex ideas of *Hogfather* was immense.

One of the things I'd always loved about Terry's writing is that it was so visual, so cinematic, and I also felt much of the dialogue should remain unchanged. Above all, I wanted to be truly faithful to the book. I wanted to be able to watch the finished film two years after the first word was written and see the book on the screen, exactly as I had imagined it from reading the text. I loved the novel so much that, frankly, I wouldn't have cared if not a single word was mine and all I'd had to do was edit what was already there. And the last thing I wanted was a screenwriter with an ego, someone who wanted to make it theirs. It's Terry Pratchett's *Hogfather* for a reason.

So my big question was: would I be able to find Terry's voice in the words that I would be shaping to bring to the screen his incredible vision of Discworld? As the development process began, I faced the inevitable challenges of having to lose several of my favourite parts of the novel for the sake of the story. I wish I'd had enough screen time for the King to give his leftovers to the peasant happy with his beany lot, and for muddy boots to be served in the restaurant. If your favourite scene or character is not included, I apologise, even if it is the God of Indigestion (against whom I have a particular gripe anyway, and so exacted an editorial revenge). But something has to give, even in the four hours that television has given us to tell the story.

So it was with trepidation that I awaited Terry's response to the first draft of the screenplay. It was with joy and relief that I greeted his first comment: 'Most of the words seem to be mine . . .' As a humble adapter, that was exactly what I wanted to hear, and that reassurance was confirmed when Colin Smythe said that Terry *wanted to give me some notes* . . .

And so, on a wonderfully sunny day in the West Country, I had the honour of a day of Terry's time, during which he made suggestions of humour, faithfulness to Discworld and yet more invention: my adaptation was 'Mucked About With' to perfection by the Creator himself. The moment when Terry said of one particular speech that even if he hadn't written it, he wished he had, will remain one of the proudest of my life – because it was one of mine. Sometime during that eight months immersed in *Hogfather* I had found a smidgeon of Terry's own voice in my own writing.

The actual broadcast film is a little different to this final shooting script – that's what happens in the cutting-room – but this at least is what we filmed. There are many people to thank who have made tremendous contributions to this adaptation, but in particular: Terry (for everything), Phil Parker, who is the best script doctor in Britain (and whose beard played a major part in convincing Terry he wasn't a suit), Elaine Pyke, our Commissioning Editor and Sarah Conroy at Sky, Lyn Holst at RHI, Rod and Ian for brilliant producing, and, most of all, my wife Susan for letting me live in Discworld for two years.

Happy Hogswatch!

Vadim Jean
Writer/Director Hogfather

Terry Pratchett's
HOGFATHER
The Illustrated Screenplay

PART ONE

WRITTEN FOR THE SCREEN

BY VADIM JEAN

MUCKED AROUND WITH

BY TERRY PRATCHETT

FINAL SHOOTING SCRIPT

INTERIOR HOUSE-DISCWORLD - NIGHT

The room is brightly decorated. Ivy and mistletoe hang
in bunches from the bookshelves. Brightly coloured
streamers festoon the walls.

NARRATOR (Voice Over)
It was the night before Hogswatch . . .

At one end there is a classic Victorian style fireside.
In the grate a fire has died down to a few sullen
ashes.

Hanging from the mantelpiece are a couple of long
stockings. Ranged along it is a selection of cards.
They have messages like 'Wishing you Joye and all Goode
Cheer at Hogswatchtime & All Through The Yeare' on
them.

A couple of the cards have pictures of a BIG JOLLY FAT
MAN carrying a sack. He is a figure clad not unlike our
own Father Christmas in red with white trimmings . . .
except with a certain hog-like quality. In one of them
he is riding in a SLEIGH drawn by four enormous HOGS.

There is a scraping noise. A few lumps of soot
thump into the ashes. The scraping becomes
louder . . . until there is a loud thump in
the fireplace.

A RED-CLOAKED FIGURE pulls itself upright
and looks around the room.

The figure looks exactly like the large
RED-CLOAKED FIGURE in the Hogswatch
cards on the mantelpiece.

It is the HOGFATHER.

He moves in a very jolly fashion across
the hearth rug, leaving sooty foot
prints behind him, to a large leather
armchair with a table by its side.

On the table is a GLASS OF SHERRY, a PORK
PIE and four TURNIPS. There is also a note.
The Hogfather reads . . .

Dere Hogfather,

*For Hogswatch I would like a toy soldier, a drum and red and white
candy cane an here is a glars of Sherre an a Pork pie for you and turnips
for Gouger an Rooter an Snot Snouter.*

The Hogfather sips the sherry, pockets both the pork
pie and the turnips and then goes back over to the
fire.

A red-gloved hand pulls presents from the sack he is
carrying and places them in the stockings hanging above
the mantelpiece: a teddy bear, a toy soldier in a
colourful uniform, a drum and a red-and-white candy
cane.

Then, as he swings the sack back over his shoulder we
see his face for the first time. It is a beamingly
jolly face, half man, half hog.

> HOGFATHER
> Ho ho ho.

And with that he ducks down, enters the chimney and
with a magical whooshing sound is gone.

EXTERIOR HOUSE–DISCWORLD/ROOF – NIGHT

The Hogfather's sleigh is ancient and runs on what look
like two felled trees side by side with the branches
still attached. By his side is a tiny, immaculately
dressed PIXIE with a perfect smile. The HOGFATHER snaps
the reins.

> HOGFATHER
> Up, Gouger! Up, Rooter! Up, Tusker! Up,
> Snouter! Giddyup!

The HOGS lurch forward and the sleigh flies off into
the night. Snow begins to fall into the PERFECT
SLEIGH TRACKS left on the roof.

EXT. GAITER'S HOUSE – NIGHT

The glow of candlelight
draws us towards one of
the windows in a Georgian
looking house. As the
CAMERA cranes closer
we hear over . . .

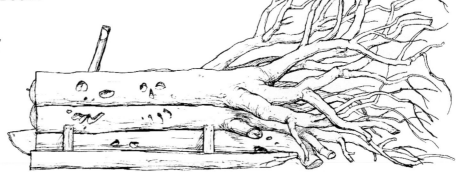

                    SUSAN (Off Camera)
          . . . and then Jack chopped down what
          was the world's last beanstalk, adding
          murder and ecological terrorism to the
          theft . . .

INT. GAITER'S HOUSE/TWYLA'S BEDROOM - NIGHT

SUSAN STO-HELIT is reading a bedtime story to two small
children, TWYLA and GAWAIN. They are about seven and
five years old respectively.

                    SUSAN
          . . . enticement and trespass charges
          already mentioned and all the giant's
          children didn't have a daddy any more
          . . .

On the cover we see the title: *Jack and the Beanstalk*.

The children are listening contentedly just their eyes
peeking over the covers.

                    SUSAN
          . . . but he got away with it and
          lived happily ever after without so
          much as a guilty twinge about what he
          had done. Which proves that you can be
          excused just about anything if you're
          a hero, because no one asks
          inconvenient questions. And now . . .

Susan closes the book with a snap.

                    SUSAN
          . . . it's time for bed.

                    TWYLA
Susan . . .

                    SUSAN
Yes?

                    TWYLA
You know last week we wrote letters to
the Hogfather?

                    SUSAN
Yes?

                    TWYLA
Well, will he really come?

There is a rustle from the other bed. Twyla's brother,
Gawain, turns over to listen surreptitiously.

                    GAWAIN
          And when's he coming here?

Susan sits down on the bed, wondering how the hell to
get through this. She pats Twyla's one visible hand and
takes a deep mental breath.

                    SUSAN
          Does it matter if you get the presents
          anyway?

                    TWYLA
          'es.

It obviously does matter. Susan tries another tack.

                    SUSAN
          Well, if you don't believe in the
          Hogfather, there won't be any presents.

                    TWYLA
          Fawt so.

Susan taps Twyla's hand and finishes tucking her in.

And with that the CAMERA pulls back through the
window, where . . .

EXT. SPACE - NIGHT

Mists roll, stars peek, glinting
faintly through.

                    NARRATOR (V.O.)
          Everything starts somewhere,
          although many physicists
          disagree. There is the constant
          desire to find out where, where
          is the point where it all began.

Gaps begin to appear in the mists and in the
distance we can just make out an odd shape.

                    NARRATOR (V.O.)
          But much, much later than that . . .
          the Discworld was formed . . .

Slowly the mists part and we begin to see the disc . . .

                    NARRATOR (V.O.)
          . . . drifting onwards through space
          atop four elephants on the shell of a
          giant turtle, The Great A'Tuin.

We begin to fly towards the Turtle.

                    NARRATOR (V.O.)
          It was some time after its creation
          when most people forgot that the very
          oldest stories of the beginning are,
          sooner or later, about blood . . .

And now we're flying through the clouds above the disc
itself.

                    NARRATOR (V.O.)
          . . . at least that's one theory . . .

Now we're skimming across the Sto Plains.

                    NARRATOR (V.O.)
          . . . The philosopher Didactylos has
          suggested an alternative hypothesis:
          'Things just happen. What the hell.'

And onwards over the city and down towards the centre . . .

                    NARRATOR (V.O.)
          And so our story begins in Ankh-
          Morpork, the twin city of proud Ankh
          and pestilent Morpork, the biggest city
          in Discworld . . .

EXT. GUILD OF ASSASSINS - NIGHT

The CAMERA flies towards a public school-like building
and glides finally to rest at the ornately carved name
above its gates . . . THE GUILD OF ASSASSINS.

                    NARRATOR (V.O.)
          . . . And is sooner, rather than
          later, about blood . . .

INT. GUILD OF ASSASSINS - NIGHT

A modest brass plaque is screwed into a wall next to a
wooden picture frame, bearing the comment 'Departed
this vale of tears on Grune 3, Year of the Sideways
Leech, with the assistance of the Hon. K. W. Dobson.'

As the CAMERA pulls out we see that we are in a wood-panelled corridor where a number of paintings and busts of the famous clients of members of the guild line the walls.

The CAMERA tracks past a glass case with a dummy wearing the ALL-BLACK UNIFORM of the Guild of Assassins and then arrives at a distinguished-looking door with an important-looking plaque: LORD DOWNEY: MASTER OF THE GUILD.

INT. LORD DOWNEY'S STUDY – NIGHT

LORD DOWNEY sits in his study catching up on the paperwork.

The study is oak-panelled and well carpeted. The furniture is very old and quite worn.

A log fire burns in the grate. There is the crackle of a shifting log. In front of it is a SLEEPING DOG.

There is no other sound but the scratching of Lord Downey's pen and the ticking of the longcase clock by the door . . . until . . . someone clears their throat.

Downey stops writing but does not raise his head.

He considers for a moment.

> LORD DOWNEY
> (businesslike)
> The doors are locked. The windows are barred. The dogs do not appear to have woken up. The squeaky floorboards haven't. I really doubt that you are a ghost and gods generally do not announce themselves so politely. You could, of course, be Death, but I don't believe he bothers with such niceties and, besides, I am feeling quite well. Hmm!

And then he looks up.

One of the AUDITORS hangs in the air.

                    LORD DOWNEY
          Good evening.

                    AUDITOR 1
          Good evening, Lord Downey.

                    LORD DOWNEY
          You appear to be a spectre.

                    AUDITOR 1
          Our nature is not a matter for
          discussion. We offer you a commission.

                    LORD DOWNEY
          You wish someone inhumed?

                    AUDITOR 1
          Brought to an end.

Downey considers for a moment.

                    LORD DOWNEY
          Our scale of fees . . .

                    AUDITOR 1
          The payment will be three million
          dollars.

Downey sits back trying unsuccessfully to hide his
surprise at the enormity of the sum.

                    LORD DOWNEY
          No questions asked, I assume?

                    AUDITOR 1
          No questions answered.

                    LORD DOWNEY
          But does the suggested fee represent
          the difficulty involved? The client is
          heavily guarded?

                    AUDITOR 1
          Not guarded at all. But almost
          certainly impossible to delete with
          conventional weapons.

Downey nods, thinking for a moment.

                    LORD DOWNEY
We like to know for whom we are
working.

                    AUDITOR 1
We are sure you do.

                    LORD DOWNEY
I mean that we need to know your name.
Or names. In strict client
confidentiality, of course.

                    AUDITOR 1
You may think of us as . . .
the Auditors.

                    LORD DOWNEY
Really? What is it you audit?

                    AUDITOR 1
Everything . . . We maintain
the logical order of the
universe.

                    LORD DOWNEY
I think we need to know a little
more than that—

                    AUDITOR 1
We are the people with three
million dollars.

Downey takes the point.

                    LORD DOWNEY
We will need to know where, when
and, of course, who.

The cowl nods.

                    AUDITOR 1
The location is not on any map. We
need the task to be completed by
sunrise tomorrow. This is essential.
As for the who . . .

A DRAWING appears on Downey's desk.

                    AUDITOR 1
Let us call him the Fat Man.

                    LORD DOWNEY
Is this a joke?

                         15

AUDITOR 1
We have no sense of humour.

LORD DOWNEY
But you do realise the consequences?

AUDITOR 1
Better than you can imagine.

Downey drums his fingers.

LORD DOWNEY
There are many who
would say this . . .
person does not exist.

AUDITOR 1
He must exist. How
else could you so
readily recognise his
picture?

Downey looks at the drawing
again. It's of . . . the
HOGFATHER.

AUDITOR 1
And many are in
correspondence with
him.

He has a point.

LORD DOWNEY
Finding him would be a
little difficult.

AUDITOR 1
You will find persons on any street who
can tell you his approximate address.

LORD DOWNEY
Yes, of course, but, as you say, I
doubt that they could give a map
reference. And even then, how could the
. . . Fat Man be inhumed? A glass of
poisoned sherry, perhaps?

The cowl has no face to crack a smile.

AUDITOR 1
You misunderstand the nature of
employment.

16

> LORD DOWNEY
> (sniffily)
> What is it that I misunderstand,
> exactly?

> AUDITOR 1
> We pay. You find the ways and means.

The cowl begins to fade.

> LORD DOWNEY
> How can I contact you?

> AUDITOR 1
> We will contact you. We know where you
> are. We know where everyone is.

The figure vanishes.

Downey stares into space for a while, and then smiles.
He picks up a speaker tube by his desk.

> LORD DOWNEY
> Winvoe, is Mister Teatime still in the
> building?

Downey picks up the picture of the Hogfather from his
desk and looks at it thoughtfully.

EXT. GAITER'S HOUSE/SUSAN'S BEDROOM – NIGHT

Frost patterns curl across the glass. As we
get closer, within we start to make out . . .

INT. GAITER'S HOUSE/SUSAN'S BEDROOM – NIGHT

Susan. She is sitting up on the bed,
reading by candlelight.

A tapping sound on the window makes her turn
her head.

Just visible through the frost is a BLACK
BEAK tapping hard at the glass.

Susan looks abruptly away.

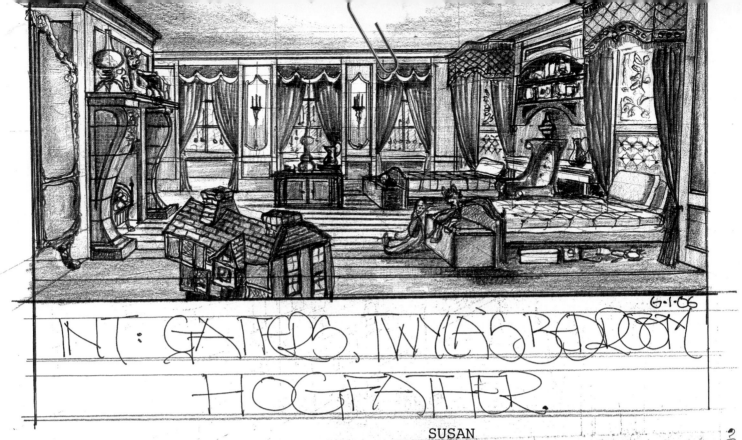

INT: GATES, TWYLA'S BEDROOM
HOGFATHER.

                    SUSAN
        Go away! I don't do that stuff anymore!

She blinks . . . then turns back to the window.

The sound of wings clatter against the glass as the
DARK OUTLINE of a BLACK BIRD flies away, its shadow
whipping across the window sill and then disappearing.

Susan sighs.

                    TWYLA (O.C.)
        Thusan?

Susan looks around.

At her door TWYLA stands barefoot in a nightdress. She
looks ridiculously cute in the slightly oversize
garment.

                    SUSAN
        (Sighing)
        Yes, Twyla?

                    TWYLA
        I'm afwaid of the monster in the
        cellar, Thusan. It's going to eat me
        up.

Susan shuts her book firmly.

                              SUSAN
          What, again?

Susan gets off the bed, trying to stay quite calm.

Twyla watches her.

Susan picks up the poker from the nursery fender and
leaves.

INT. GAITER'S HOUSE/BACK STAIRS - NIGHT

SUSAN goes down the back stairs, with TWYLA following
her. We hear muffled voices coming from the direction
of the dining room. As they creep past, the door opens.

                         GUEST'S VOICE
          Ye gawds, there's a gel out here with a
          poker!

She sees figures silhouetted in the light and we make
out a worried older female face.

                          MRS GAITER
          Susan? Er . . . what are you doing?

Susan looks at the poker and then back at the woman.

                              SUSAN
          Twyla said she's afraid of a monster in
          the cellar, Mrs Gaiter.

And then another face smoking a BIG CIGAR appears
alongside MRS GAITER's.

                          MR GAITER
          And yer going to attack it with a
          poker, eh?

Cigar smoke wafts out from the room.

                              SUSAN
          Yes.

Mrs Gaiter raises her voice so the guests behind can
hear.

                          MRS GAITER
          Susan's our governess.

There is a change in the expression on the faces
peering out from the dining room to amused respect.

GUEST
She beats up monsters with a poker?

MR GAITER
Actually, that's a very clever idea. Me
daughter gets it into her head there's
a monster in the cellar, you go in with
the poker and make a few bashing noises
while the child listens, and then
everything's all right.

MRS GAITER
Is that what you're doing, Susan?

SUSAN
Yes, Mrs Gaiter.

MR GAITER
This I've got to watch, by Io! It's not
every day you see monsters beaten up by
a gel.

There is a swish of silk and a cloud of cigar
smoke as the diners pour out into the hall.

INT. GAITER'S HOUSE/HALL - NIGHT

TWYLA sits demurely at the top of the cellar
stairs, hugging her knees.

On the Guests' faces. Suddenly we hear a door
opened and shut. Then silence. Then a
terrifying scream. One woman faints and a Guest
drops his cigar.

TWYLA
(calmly)
You don't have to worry, everything
will be all right. She always wins.

There are thuds and clangs, and then a whirring noise,
and finally a sort of bubbling.

Susan pushes open the door. The poker is bent at right
angles.

There is nervous applause.

MR GAITER
Ver' well done. Ver' persykological.

Clever idea, that, bendin' the poker.
And I expect you're not afraid any
more, eh, my girl?

                    TWYLA
No.

                    MR GAITER
Ver' persykological.

                    TWYLA
Susan says don't get afraid, get angry.

                    MRS GAITER
Er, thank you, Susan.

MRS GAITER is now a trembling bouquet of nerves.

                    MRS GAITER
And, er, now, if you'd all like to come
back into the parlour - I mean, the
drawing room.

Susan watches the party as they make their way back up
the hall.

                    MR GAITER (O.C.)
Dashed convincin', the way she bent the
poker like that—

And the door shuts.

Susan waits.

                    SUSAN
Have they all gone, Twyla?

                    TWYLA
Yes, Susan.

                    SUSAN
Good.

Susan goes back into the cellar.

Twyla waits until . . .

 . . . Susan emerges towing something large and hairy.
She hauls it up the steps by the tail . . .

INT. GAITER'S HOUSE/PASSAGE - NIGHT

. . . and down the other passage . . .

EXT. GAITER'S HOUSE/BACK YARD - NIGHT

. . . to the back yard, where she kicks it out.

> SUSAN
> That's what we do to monsters.

Twyla watches carefully.

> SUSAN
> And now it's back to bed for you, my
> girl.

INT. LORD DOWNEY'S STUDY - NIGHT

There is a knock at the door. He pushes his paperwork
aside and sits back.

> LORD DOWNEY
> Come in, Mister Teatime.

The door opens . . . but it's CARTER, one of the
Guild's servants, carefully balancing a tea tray.

> LORD DOWNEY
> Ah, Carter. Just put it on the table
> over there, will you?

> CARTER
> Yes, sir. Sorry, sir, I'll go and fetch
> another cup directly, sir.

> LORD DOWNEY
> What?

> CARTER
> For your visitor, sir.

> LORD DOWNEY
> What visitor? Oh, when Mister Teati—

He stops. He turns.

There is a young man sitting on the hearthrug, playing
with the dogs.

                    LORD DOWNEY
            Mister Teatime!

                    TEATIME
            It's pronounced Teh-ah-
            time-eh, sir. Everyone gets
            it wrong, sir.

                    LORD DOWNEY
            How did you do get in
            here?

                    TEATIME
            Easily, sir. I got
            mildly scorched on the
            last few feet, of
            course.

Downey sees some lumps of soot
on the hearthrug. And then, with a 'how
the hell did he do that?' look on his face, glances
at the fireplace.

TEATIME's face is fresh, open and friendly. It is
topped by curly hair. The face is actually quite
pretty, in a boyish sort of way . . . and hasn't
stopped smiling since it arrived. But then he turns
from the profile we've seen him in up to now and
realise for the first time that . . .

    . . . he only has ONE EYE. The missing orb has been
replaced by a ball of glass.

Downey looks a little closer and seems disconcerted.

In close on Teatime's face we can see that the other
'good' eye has the smallest and sharpest pupil you have
ever seen - practically a pin-hole.

Downey retreats behind his desk again.

                    LORD DOWNEY
            The dogs seem to like you.

                    TEATIME
            I get on well with animals, sir.

Downey nods and looks down at an open file on his desk.

                    LORD DOWNEY
            I have a report here that says you
            nailed Sir George's dog to the ceiling.

                    TEATIME
          Couldn't have it barking while I was
          working, sir.

                    LORD DOWNEY
          Some people would have drugged it.

                    TEATIME
          Oh.

Teatime looks despondent for a moment, but then he
brightens.

                    TEATIME
          But I definitely fulfilled the
          contract, sir. I checked Sir George's
                    breathing with a mirror as
                    instructed. It's in my
                    report.

          He pauses before reading on.

                    LORD DOWNEY
          Apparently the man's head
          was several feet from his
          body at that point.

          Teatime appears to see nothing
          incongruous about this, his smile
          still beaming.

                    TEATIME
               (anxiously)
          That was all right, wasn't
          it, sir?

                    LORD DOWNEY
          It, uh . . . lacked
          elegance.

                    TEATIME
          Ah. Thank you, sir. I am always happy
          to be corrected. I shall remember that
          next time, sir.

Downey takes a deep breath.

                    LORD DOWNEY
          It is about the next time that I wish
          to talk.

He holds up the picture of the Hogfather and looks at it.

                              24

> LORD DOWNEY
> As a matter of interest, how
> would you go about inhuming
> . . .

Downey turns the picture so that
Teatime can see it.

> LORD DOWNEY
> . . . this . . .
> gentleman?

Teatime leans forward, with a
curious intent expression.

> TEATIME
> Difficult, sir.

> LORD DOWNEY
> Certainly.

> TEATIME
> But I have devoted some time to it,
> sir.

Downey stops, and then looks shocked.

> LORD DOWNEY
> You've actually sat down and thought
> out how to inhume the Hogfather?

> TEATIME
> Oh, yes, sir. And the Soul Cake Duck.
> And the Sandman. And Death, sir.

Downey blinks again.

> LORD DOWNEY
> But they're imaginary creatures?

> TEATIME
> Yes, sir. Makes it a challenge.

Downey drums his fingers on the desk again.

> TEATIME
> I suppose I just see things differently
> from other people.

Downey looks directly at Teatime.

                    LORD DOWNEY
         Well . . . we might be able to see the
         complaint of Sir George's estate
         against you with regard to his dogs
         rather differently . . .

Teatime's one good eye flickers with interest.

                    LORD DOWNEY
          . . . and approve your graduation to
         full membership of the Guild . . .

                    TEATIME
         'Take the dark', sir? Wear . . .
         black, sir?

                    LORD DOWNEY
          . . . if you agree to undertake this
         contract . . . with due elegance, of
         course.

                    TEATIME
         With elegance guaranteed, sir.

Teatime turns and starts to leave.

                    LORD DOWNEY
         Mister uh . . . Teh-ah-time-eh.

Teatime stops.

                    LORD DOWNEY
         I want to be quite certain about this.
         You . . . have . . . actually applied
         . . . yourself to a study of ways of
         killing Death?

                    TEATIME
         Only as a hobby, sir.

                    LORD DOWNEY
         And yet . . . some people might say
         that he is technically immortal.

                    TEATIME
         Everyone has their weak point, sir.

Downey stares at him. Teatime smiles as he leaves.

INT. DEATH'S HOUSE/LIFETIMERS ROOM – NIGHT

The room is like a vast library with canyon-like

rows of shelves that go as high as you can see. It is
dark. Skulls decorate the ends of the cases.

Lining the shelves are rows of LIFETIMERS, like egg
timers made of wood and brass and glass. In DEATH's
house everything is in BLACK AND WHITE. (Only living
things are in colour in his domain.)

A few grains of sand fall in slow motion through the
glass of one. Just as the last grains of sand fall, a
SKELETAL HAND picks it up.

The Lifetimer slips into the depths of a dark CLOAK.

A SWORD HANDLE slots into a black scabbard.

DEATH's other skeletal hand grips a black SCYTHE handle
. . .

   . . . a silver SADDLE is thrown onto the back of a
WHITE HORSE and . . .

   . . . and a blue glowing SCYTHE BLADE sweeps through
the air.

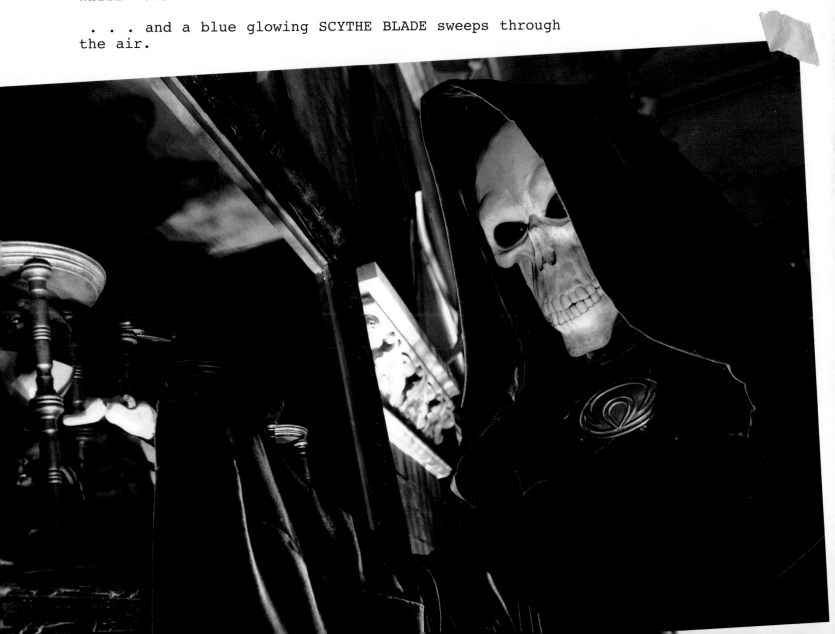

INT. THE MENDED DRUM – NIGHT

Three men are sat round a table in a snug, lit by a
candle stuck in a saucer. By their appearance and
demeanour you would say they were criminals.

CHICKENWIRE, a scrawny man, is twisting a napkin
between his hands like a garotte.

> CHICKENWIRE
> 's gone six. He ain't coming. Let's go.

An open bottle of beer is taken from a tray and placed
down in front of him. Chickenwire picks up the bottle
and takes care to keep it away from the candle flame as
he sits down.

> MEDIUM DAVE
> Sit down, will you? Assassins are
> always fashionably late. 'Cos of style,
> right?

MEDIUM DAVE is a solid-looking man with a thoughtful
        expression on his face. Another bottle is placed
        in front of him.

> CHICKENWIRE
> What's this? You never said he
> was an Assassin.

> Another bottle is placed in front of
> BANJO.

> MEDIUM DAVE
> It's Teatime. He's paying top
> rates. We can wait for top
> rates.

> CHICKENWIRE
> Teatime? I've heard he's . . .

> He waves his hands vaguely, trying to
> find the right word.

> CHICKENWIRE
> . . . mental. And
> he's got a funny eye.

> There is a sound like
> distant thunder. It is
> Banjo Lilywhite clearing
> his throat. He is an
> enormous man for whom

breathing is an intellectual exercise. He has one
blocked nostril and his mouth is open all the time, as
though he lives on invisible plankton.

                    BANJO
          What I don' unnerstan is, how longaz
          diz place had waiters?

There is a blur, and a knife shudders in the table
between Chickenwire's thumb and index finger.

He looks down at it in horror.

                    VOICE (O.C.)
          Good evening.

The 'waiter' puts down the tray.

The group stares at him in silence.

He gives them a friendly smile. He has a glass eye.
It's Teatime.

Chickenwire tries to look straight at him but quickly
looks away.

With a sudden whirl of movement that makes the men
start, Teatime spins away, grabs a chair, swings it
up to the table and sits down on it.

                    TEATIME
          Do have another drink while we
          wait for the other members of our
          little troupe.

Medium Dave's lips start to frame the
opening letters of 'Who . . .'
Chickenwire kicks Medium Dave's leg
under the table.

INT. GAITER'S HOUSE/SUSAN'S BEDROOM - NIGHT

Susan settles down with her
book once more.

Then . . . the door is pushed
open. It reveals the tousled
shape of Twyla, hanging onto
the doorknob with one hand.

> TWYLA
> Susan, there's a monster under my bed
> again . . .

The click of Susan's fingernails stops.

She sighs.

INT. GAITER'S HOUSE/TWYLA'S BEDROOM - NIGHT

TWYLA leaps into bed from a distance as a precaution
against claws.

There is a metallic tzing! as SUSAN withdraws the bent
poker from the little brass stand it shares with the
tongs and the coal shovel.

She leans over as if to tuck Twyla up. Then her hand
darts down and under the bed. She grabs a handful of
hair and pulls.

Before the bogeyman can get its balance, it's spread-
eagled against the wall with one arm behind its back.

Twyla and GAWAIN bounce up and down on their beds.

> TWYLA
> Do the Voice on it! Do the Voice on
> it!

> THE BOGEYMAN
> Not the Voice!

> TWYLA
> Hit it on the head with the poker!

> THE BOGEYMAN
> Not the poker!

> SUSAN
> This is a friendly warning, understand?
> Because it's Hogswatch.

> THE BOGEYMAN
> You a witch or something?

> SUSAN
> I'm just . . . something. Now . . .
> you won't be around here again, will
> you? Or we'll put your head under the
> blanket. It's got fluffy bunnies on it.

THE BOGEYMAN
Not the . . .

SUSAN
GO AWAY AND STOP BOTHERING ME.

The BOGEYMAN's POV of Susan's face as just for
a moment he sees a flash of BARED SKULL. He
runs like hell.

TWYLA
That wasn't as much fun as the
one last month. You know, when
you kicked him in the
trousers.

SUSAN
Just go to sleep now.

INT. THE MENDED DRUM - NIGHT

The entrance door opens slightly. A
figure comes in, but only just. It
inserts itself in the gap and
sidles along the wall in a
manner calculated not to
attract attention . . . but of
course it does.

The gang are looking over at
him.

It looks at them over its
turned-up collar.

CHICKENWIRE
That's a wizard.

The figure hurries over and drags
up a chair. It's MR SIDENEY.

MR SIDENEY
(hissing)
No I'm not! I'm incognito!

MEDIUM DAVE
Right, you're just someone
in a pointy hat. This is
my brother Banjo, this is
Chick—

33

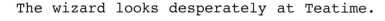

The wizard looks desperately at Teatime.

                    MR SIDENEY
          I didn't want to come!

                    TEATIME
          Mr Sideney here is indeed a wizard. A
          student, anyway. But down on his luck
          at the moment, hence his willingness to
          join us on this venture.

                    CHICKENWIRE
          So what's the job?

                    TEATIME
          We don't do jobs. We perform services.
          And the service will earn each of you
          ten thousand dollars.

                    MEDIUM DAVE
          That's a lot more'n Thieves' Guild
          rate.

                    TEATIME
          I've never liked the Thieves' Guild.

                    MEDIUM DAVE
          Why not?

                    TEATIME
          They ask too many questions.

                    MEDIUM DAVE
              (quickly)
          We don't ask questions.

          The gang work it out . . . CHICKENWIRE
          looks at SIDENEY.

                    CHICKENWIRE
          No one said anything about there
          being magic in all this.

                    MEDIUM DAVE
          Exactly how far down on his luck?

          The wizard tries not to meet anyone's gaze.

                    TEATIME
              (cheerfully)
          Chrysoprase the troll has this odd
          little thing about money that turns
          into lead the next day. And so, funnily

does Archchancellor Ridcully of the
Unseen University. So our friend needs
to earn a little cash in a hurry and
in a climate where arms and legs stay
on.

                    CHICKENWIRE
No one said anything about arms and
legs going missing.

                    TEATIME
Our destination is . . . a place where
no one ever dies.

Chickenwire looks relieved, if perplexed.

                    CHICKENWIRE
Where is this place?

Teatime turns and smiles at him.

                    TEATIME
If I'm paying you, why isn't it me
who's asking the questions?

Chickenwire doesn't even try to outstare the
glass eye a second time.

                    MEDIUM DAVE
        Locks?

Teatime looks at Medium Dave with tried patience
all over his face.

                    TEATIME
We have a locksmith.

                    MEDIUM DAVE
        Who?

Teatime nods.

                    TEATIME
Mr Brown.

The group all nod with recognition and
approval. And as they do, a bag of tools
is heaved onto the table.

                    MR BROWN
And you can help me carry this.
It's rather heavy.

MR BROWN, the wiry, bald, bespectacled man, takes a seat.

Teatime turns and looks up at the bulk that is Banjo.

>   TEATIME
>   What is this?

>   MEDIUM DAVE
>   This is Banjo, my brother.

Medium Dave rolls himself a cigarette.

>   TEATIME
>   Does it do tricks?

Time stands still for a moment. The other men look at Medium Dave.

The look on Medium Dave's face could kill. His fingers apparently calmly tuck the tobacco into a cigarette paper and raise it to his lips.

>   MEDIUM DAVE
>   No.

>   CHICKENWIRE
>   He can lift two men in each hand. By
>   their necks.

>   BANJO
>   Yur.

>   TEATIME
>   He looks like a volcano.

>   MEDIUM DAVE
>   Really?

And Medium Dave is up.

>   MEDIUM DAVE
>   Wanna be fashionably late, do ya?

Chickenwire reaches out hastily and pushes Dave back down in his seat.

Teatime turns and smiles at him.

>   TEATIME
>   I do so hope we're going to be friends,
>   Mr Medium Dave. It really hurts to
>   think I might not be among friends.

He gives him another bright smile. Then he turns back to the rest of the table and looks Banjo up and down.

>   TEATIME
>   Then I suppose we might as well make a
>   start.

And he hits Banjo very hard in the mouth.

INT. YMPA/BANJO'S ROOM - NIGHT

Banjo is asleep. He snores in and, as he breathes out, his lips flap open to reveal A GAP IN HIS FRONT TEETH.

The CAMERA tracks across his pillow and down to the space between it and the sheet to reveal . . .

. . . his TOOTH in big close-up.

Then a young female hand appears and picks up the tooth from under his pillow.

>   VIOLET (O.C.)
>   (whispering)
>   My name's Violet and I will be your
>   Tooth Fairy for this evening.

Then in one deft movement she starts to put a SHINY SILVER HALF-DOLLAR in the place of the Tooth. But suddenly the coin drops from her fingers.

Banjo's eyes open. He looks up.

. . . a hand clamps over VIOLET BOTTLER's mouth. All we can see are her terrified eyes and her MOP OF RED HAIR as she drops out of shot.

EXT. STREET/ANKH MORPORK - NIGHT

A CART trundles through the freezing foggy streets, the driver, ERNIE, hunched in his seat. He seems to be all big thick brown overcoat.

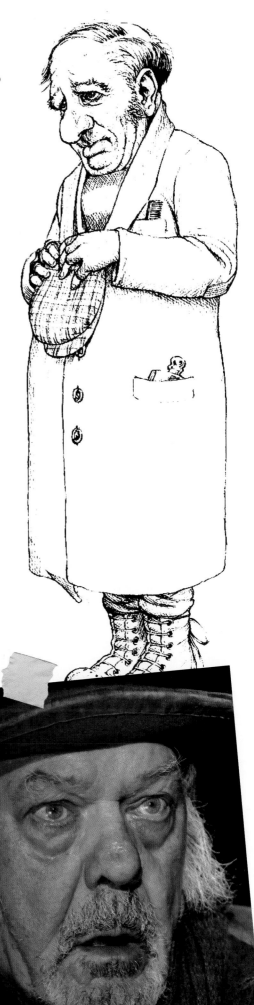

On the side of the cart in elegant sign writing is a
picture of a wide child's grin with one tooth missing.
Beneath it is written:

Tooth Fairy Bulk Collection: WORKING TOGETHER FOR A
BRIGHTER SMILE.

A figure darts out of the swirls of fog and is suddenly
on the box next to him.

Ernie stops and stiffens abruptly.

The point of a KNIFE penetrates through four layers of
thick clothing and stops just at the point where it
pricks the flesh.

>   ERNIE
>   Er - there ain't nothing valuable,
>   y'know, nothing valuable, only a few
>   bags of . . .

>   TEATIME
>   Teeth, I know. My name's Teh-ah-time-
>   eh. What is your name, sir?

>   ERNIE
>   Ernie. Er. Ernie. Yes. Ernie.

Teatime turns his head
slightly.

>   TEATIME
>   Come along,
>   gentlemen. This is my
>   friend Ernie. He's
>   going to be our
>   driver for tonight.

Ernie sees the gang emerge
from the fog and head for
the cart. Banjo carries a
long bundle over his
shoulder. The bundle moves
and makes muffled noises.
Sticking out of one end is
a mop of red hair.

The group clamber into the
cart behind him. Ernie
doesn't turn to look at
them.

Teatime withdraws the knife. Ernie stops holding his
breath and lets out an audible noise.

> ERNIE
> I ain't rightly allowed to carry
> passengers, see, Charlie'll give me a
> right telling-off . . .

> TEATIME
> Oh, don't you worry about that.

Teatime slaps Ernie on the back.

> TEATIME
> We're all friends here!

Banjo can't take his eyes off
Violet in the carpet.

> BANJO
> Our mam said no hittin'
> girls. Only bad boys do
> that, our mam said!

> TEATIME
> Shssh! Ernie here
> doesn't want to listen
> to our troubles.

Teatime does not take his
gaze off the driver as the
cart begins to clatter across
the cobbles.

> ERNIE
> Where to, mister?

> TEATIME
> You know the way, Ernie.
> Behind the Unseen University, I think.

EXT. BEHIND THE UNSEEN UNIVERSITY - NIGHT

The road here is deserted, despite the bustle of the
city behind them and the bulk of the University nearby.

The cart trundles past the University's rubbish pits
where a sign reads: THE UNSEEN UNIVERSITY SPELL DUMP.

> ERNIE
> (muttering)
> Bloody wizards.

In the back of the cart MR SIDENEY ducks down suddenly
out of sight.

                    MEDIUM DAVE
      You incognito again?

                    MR SIDENEY
    I . . . dropped a spell.

EXT. STREET/ANKH MORPORK - NIGHT

The cart is heading towards the wall at the end of a
dead-end street. Half-collapsed houses, windows
smashed, doors stolen, lean against one another on
either side.

                    ERNIE
      'ere, I can't take you lot through the
      wall.

                    TEATIME
       (sighing)
      Listen, Ernie . . . Ern . . . you will
      take us through or, and I say this with
      very considerable regret, I will have
      to kill you.

                    ERNIE
      But if'n I take you through—

                    TEATIME
      What's the worst that can happen?
      You'll lose your job. Whereas if you
      don't, you'll die. So if you look at it
      like that, we're actually doing you a
      favour. Oh, do say yes.

                    ERNIE
      Er . . . yes.

Moments later . . .

On a small tin, rather like a snuff-box. Ernie's hand
opens it. There is glowing dust inside.

                    TEATIME
      So . . . you don't need any special
      training or anything?

                    ERNIE
      Er . . . you just chucks it at the
      wall there and it goes twing.

                    TEATIME
        Really? May I try?

Teatime takes the tin from his unresisting hand and
throws a pinch of dust into the air in front of the
horse. It hovers for a moment and then produces a
narrow, glittering arch in the air. It sparkles and
goes . . .

    . . . *twing*.

                    BANJO
        Aw, innat nice, eh, our Davey?

                MEDIUM DAVE
        Yeah.

                    TEATIME
        And then you just drive forward?

            ERNIE
        That's right. Quick,
        mind. It only stays
        open for a little
        while.

Teatime pockets the little
tin.

            TEATIME
        Thank you very much,
        Ernie. Very much
        indeed.

His other hand lashes out.
There is a glint of metal.

Ernie blinks, and then falls
sideways off his seat.

            TEATIME
        Wasn't he dull?

Teatime picks up the reins
and drives the cart towards
the wall where . . . it
passes through the soft
place.

Snow begins to fall . . . on
the recumbent shape of
Ernie.

It also falls through the materialising AUDITORS.

                    AUDITOR 1
Well, we are frankly impressed.

                    AUDITOR 2
Indeed, we would never have thought of
doing it this way.

                    AUDITOR 1
Going to the Tooth Fairy's Castle
. . .

                    AUDITOR 3
To destroy children's belief.

                    AUDITOR 4
Who would have thought it?

                    AUDITOR 2
If the innocent young things don't
believe . . . then there is no
Hogfather.

It stops. A dark shape is approaching
through the snow.

                    AUDITOR 4
It's him.

They fade hurriedly - not quite vanishing,
but spreading out and thinning until they
are lost in the background.

The dark figure is DEATH. From his skeletal
face, blue-illuminated eyes throw points of
light in front of him.

He stops by Ernie and pulls a Lifetimer out
of his cloak. He looks at it, puts it back
and then reaches down.

                    DEATH
COULD I GIVE YOU A HAND?

Ernie looks up gratefully.

                    ERNIE
    Cor, yeah.

He gets to his feet, swaying a little.

ERNIE
Here, your fingers're cold, mister!

DEATH
SORRY.

ERNIE
What'd he go and do that for? I did
what he said. He could've killed me.

Ernie feels inside his overcoat
and pulls out a small and, at
this point, strangely transparent
silver flask.

ERNIE
I always keep a nip on me
these cold nights. Keeps
me spirits up.

DEATH
YES INDEED.

DEATH looks around briefly and
sniffs the air. He turns and
catches a glimpse of the last
SPARKLES around the outline of the
narrow glittering ARCH in the wall
as it fades to nothing with a final
twing.

ERNIE
How'm I going to explain all this then,
eh?

Ernie takes a pull from the flask.

DEATH
SORRY? THAT WAS VERY RUDE OF
ME. I WASN'T PAYING
ATTENTION.

ERNIE
I said, what'm I going to
tell people? Letting some
blokes ride off with my cart
neat as you like . . .
That's gonna be the sack for
sure . . .

DEATH
AH. WELL. THERE AT LEAST I
HAVE SOME GOOD NEWS, ERNEST.

Ernie listens and then looks at the corpse at his feet.

                    DEATH
          AND, THEN AGAIN, I ALSO HAVE SOME BAD
          NEWS.

Ernie looks back up at the seven-foot skeleton with a
scythe.

                    ERNIE
          So I'm dead, then.

                    DEATH
          CORRECT.

It sinks in for Ernie.

                    DEATH
          NOW THESE . . . BLOKES . . . ?

But before Ernie can say anything he disappears.
And with a shrug of his shoulders DEATH walks
away, leaving the street empty, except for the
fleshy abode of the late Ernie.

The grey shapes come back into focus.

                    AUDITOR 2
          Honestly, he gets worse and worse. He
          acts as if he likes people.

                    AUDITOR 3
          Yes . . . but the beauty of this
          plan is that he can't interfere.

                    AUDITOR 4
          He can go everywhere.

                    AUDITOR 1
          No. Not quite everywhere.

          And, with ineffable smugness, the Auditors
          turn and look towards the wall where the
          cart has passed through.

          As it starts to snow quite heavily the CAMERA
          TRACKS slowly towards and then 'through' the
          wall into WHITE . . .

INT. TOOTH FAIRY'S CASTLE/FOOT OF TOWER - NIGHT

The CAMERA emerges from white to reveal . . .

. . . the peaceful and quiet vast central entrance hall. The walls are white marble and stone. Long sweeping stairs wind their way up the central tower, which seems to go on forever.

A GUARD near the door is picking his nose. He inspects the finger. As he does we see that the badge on his chest has a TOOTH SYMBOL on it. As he looks up, his expression changes to one of horror and his eyes start to bulge. But this is not the bogey from hell . . .

Chickenwire is on his back and, moving like lightning, has tightened a wire around the guard's neck as we discover where his name comes from.

There is a dull thud as the guard slumps to the floor.

Sat on the bottom steps of the staircases are two lightly armed guards wearing TOOTH-SHAPED HELMETS.

> TOOTH GUARD 1
> It's a great job but you look a right
> tit in these helmets.

Just as the other guard nods Banjo grabs them by the scruff of their necks and lifts them off the ground.

Their legs struggle as they adjust their helmets just in time for Banjo to bang their heads together and they collapse in a heap on the floor.

Chickenwire has his arms around another guard. Medium Dave spits on his fist and punches the guard in the kidneys.

The guard's pale face is frozen in a rictus of pain. Then he crumples into a heap of limbs that rolls down the steps until it reaches the bottom and is still. Slowly it evaporates . . .

Looking on, Teatime smiles.

EXT. ROOF TOPS/ANKH-MORPORK - NIGHT

As far as we can see are the snow-capped rooftops of
Ankh-Morpork. In the distance we see what appears to be
a body falling and hitting one of the roofs. And then
another . . . and another . . . and another.

INT. DEATH'S HOUSE/LIFETIMERS ROOM - NIGHT

DEATH picks up a LIFETIMER. The last few grains of sand
are running out. He puts it inside his robes and is
about to move away when he sees that the one next to it
on the same shelf is also expiring.

He picks that one up too.
Then he sees that there are
several in this area all
about to run out. He stops,
straightens. Something's
happening and it's not quite
right.

From an adjacent room there
is a surge in the sound of
falling sand.

DEATH looks round . . .

. . . as ALBERT, DEATH's
67-year-old small, hunched
assistant, also roused by
the sound, puts his head
around the door. He is
carrying a FRYING PAN with
BACON and EGGS in it.
Albert too looks towards
the adjacent room,
worried.

                    DEATH
        SOMETHING IS NOT
    RIGHT, ALBERT.

Albert shrugs his shoulders.

                RAVEN (O.C.)
        Too right.

Albert and DEATH turn to see that the RAVEN is looking
behind them . . . They look to where he is looking.

One of the shelves of Lifetimers swings open like a

door to reveal the adjacent room . . .

INT. GAITER'S HOUSE/SCHOOL ROOM - NIGHT

The city's clocks strike six in the distance.

Susan is tidying up the schoolroom and getting things
ready for the morning. She picks up the things the
children have left lying on the floor and looks around
the room.

There are two stockings hanging from the mantelpiece of
the small schoolroom grate . . .

. . . Twyla's paintings, all blobby blue skies,
violently green grass and red houses with four square
windows . . .

She straightens up and stares at them, her fingernails
beating a thoughtful tattoo on a wooden pencil case.

The CAMERA tracks in to TWYLA's PAINTING . . . towards
one of the child-like houses and right into the doorway
as we . . .

                                         DISSOLVE TO:

INT. TOOTH FAIRY'S CASTLE/ STAIRS - DAY

Inside the castle where another
guard runs for his life up the
staircase until he stops in his
tracks. His face turns white as
he looks up.

Teatime stands over him . . .
and smiles.

> TEATIME
> Hello. My name's Teh-ah-
> time-eh. What's yours?

The guard's face turns even
whiter.

Teatime's hand moves with
incredible speed and a flash of
silver blade . . .

Teatime smiles.

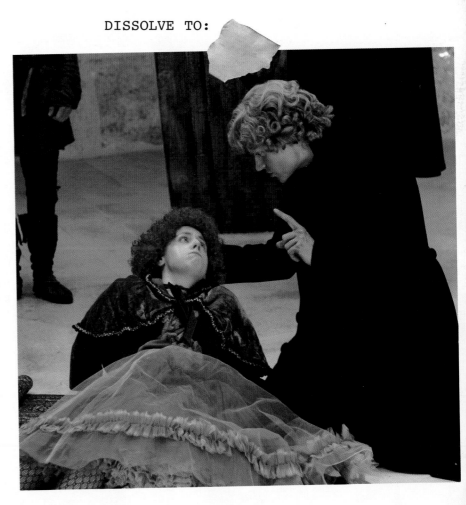

INT. GAITER'S HOUSE/SCHOOL ROOM – NIGHT

On Susan. She is looking at Twyla's painting. It is as if she has watched something terrible.

INT. TOOTH FAIRY'S CASTLE/FOOT OF TOWER – DAY

Banjo gently lays the roll of carpet on the floor. He steps back. As he does Teatime nods to Medium Dave who steps forward, takes hold of one end of the roll and pulls hard.

The roll unravels and Violet Bottler is unfurled across the white stone. She rolls to a stop looking rather pale.

> VIOLET
> I don't know what you're expecting me
> to say but I'm tel—

A hand clamps over her mouth. Teatime is crouched by her.

> TEATIME
> Questions first, babble later.

Teatime pulls her head up by the mop of red hair.

> TEATIME
> Now, Miss Bottler. I'd like you to
> think of me as a friend . . .

INT. DEATH'S HOUSE/LIFETIMERS SECRET ROOM – NIGHT

DEATH walks into the secret room. It's smaller than the main Lifetimers room (merely the size of a cathedral!) and DEATH looks at another row of Lifetimers.

But these are . . . different . . . these look as though they are made of highlights and shadows with no real substance at all. They have labels on them. The larger ones have the names of the gods on them. The smaller ones . . .

A bony hand runs along the labels: The Tooth Fairy – The Sandman – John Barleycorn – The Soul Cake Duck . . . and then THE HOGFATHER.

DEATH leans towards it and looks more closely at the Hogfather Lifetimer. The SAND is running so fast we can

see the level dropping. When he looks up, he appears,
if a skull can be otherwise, even more mortified . . .

                        DEATH
          OH DEAR.

Behind him . . .

                  ALBERT
          . . . dear, dear.

Death turns to his assistant.

                        DEATH
                  WE MAY NOT HAVE MUCH
                  TIME, ALBERT.

INT. TOOTH FAIRY'S
CASTLE/DISPLAY CASE
ROOM 1 - DAY

Violet is sat on the floor
tied to the leg of an
exhibition case. She has a
neckerchief tied around her
mouth. Teatime is smiling at
her and then looks up at the
gathered gang.

Behind him range long lines
of museum-like exhibition
cabinets. He leads the gang
down the aisle. Chickenwire
looks into one of the cases.
It is packed full of teeth.

                  CHICKENWIRE
          Teeth?

                  TEATIME
          What did you expect in the Tooth
          Fairy's castle?

                  CHICKENWIRE
          Gives me the creeps just thinking about
          it.

                  TEATIME
          You don't have to think. You just have
          to do what I said.

                    MEDIUM DAVE
        All of them?

                    TEATIME
        Every last one.

                    CHICKENWIRE
        But that's millions.

                    TEATIME
        And Mr Brown, I want you to unlock
        every door you can find.

    Mr Brown nods grumpily and heads off.

    Medium Dave goes over to Teatime confidentially.

                    MEDIUM DAVE
        What's this really all about?

Teatime gestures to Banjo, who is stood by himself
staring at a case, and steps close to Medium Dave's
face.

> TEATIME
> Does he believe in things like the Soul
> Cake Duck, the Sandman and the Tooth
> Fairy?

> MEDIUM DAVE
> Yes, even the Hogfather.

> TEATIME
> Well, after we're finished here, not
> even he will.

And with that Teatime turns. With one lightning
movement he plunges his knife into the glass of one of
the cases.

With a sickening crunch tiny teeth begin to trickle
onto the floor.

EXT. THE CASTLE OF BONES - NIGHT

DEATH rides a large white horse, BINKY, across the sky.

> DEATH
> ONWARDS, BINKY.

Binky skims the tops of the fir trees as the icy
landscape beneath him rises into a snow-covered
mountain range.

As the horse climbs we begin to see the outline of a
snow-covered structure that seems to be almost sculpted
out of the mountain side.

The pillars at the entrance are hundreds of feet high.
Each of the steps leading up is taller than a man. They
are the grey-green of old ice. Ice. Not bone. There are
faintly familiar shapes to the pillars, possibly a
suggestion of femur or skull, but it is made of ice:
THE HOGFATHER'S CASTLE OF BONES.

Binky flies down towards it. As we get closer we can
see that there is something inside the entrance to the
castle. In front of it, a blur of pink moves towards
the forest . . .

INT. THE CASTLE OF BONES/ENTRANCE - NIGHT

Binky doesn't quite fly up the high stairs, more walks
on a ground level of his own devising, into the
building. Beneath the columns is the HOGFATHER'S
SLEIGH, with HOGS, snuffling the snow in front of it.

There is a slash of oxblood-red colour draped across
the seat.

A sound behind him makes DEATH turn. The PIXIE HELPER
(from scene 2 with the Hogfather) is staggering out
from inside the Castle of Bones, DRUNK and dishevelled.
He takes a swig from one of two SHERRY GLASSES.

>   PIXIE HELPER
> Wey hey! First Hogswatch off in a
> thousand years. Even if I'm going to
> have the mother of all hangovers in the
> morning.

Then he sees DEATH and stops in his tracks. He looks at
the glasses, then back up to DEATH and then runs like
hell.

DEATH watches him go and then turns back to the sleigh.

Closer now, he sees that the red is the HOGFATHER'S
COSTUME on the Hogfather's sleigh but there is no
Hogfather.

DEATH looks up.

Something is fleeing through the forest. There is a
flash of what could be pink flesh. As it runs, the
sounds become more and more animal-like.

DEATH's bony fingers drum a thinking ripple of tapping
on the ice-frosted handle of his scythe . . .

INT. GAITER'S HOUSE/TWYLA'S BEDROOM - NIGHT

Susan is sat on the bed in mid-debate with the
children.

>   GAWAIN
> And how can the Hogfather bring all the
> presents to everyone all at the same
> time?

>   TWYLA
> Unless there are lots of Hogfathers . . .

                    SUSAN
Look, you've always believed in the
Hogfather, yes?

                    TWYLA
Yes.

                    SUSAN
Well, if you don't believe in him he
won't come down the chimney.

Twyla looks unconvinced.

                    TWYLA
It's a very small chimney.

                    SUSAN
And a very small stocking if you don't
go to sleep.

As Susan tucks Twyla in there is a flicker of
concern across her face. What HAS got into
them?

INT. VIRGINIA PROOD'S HOUSE/BEDROOM - NIGHT

A MOUSE peeks its nose out of a hole
in a skirting board. It scurries
along the wall and then stops in
front of . . . a MOUSE TRAP. It has
been baited with a piece of pork
crackling. A brief scurry and its
jaw closes on the rind. Or, rather,
passes through it.

The mouse looks around at what is
now lying under the big spring . . .

Then its head turns to the BLACK-
CLAD FIGURE that has faded into
view by the wainscoting.

                    MOUSE
Squeak?

            DEATH OF RATS
SQUEAK.

And with that, the mouse leaves its still
body in the trap.

The DEATH OF RATS looks around the room with interest.

It is brightly decorated. Ivy and mistletoe hang in bunches from the bookshelves. Brightly coloured streamers festoon the walls.

The Death of Rats leaps onto a chair and from there on to the table and into a glass of SHERRY, which tips over and breaks. A puddle spreads around four TURNIPS and begins to soak into a note which has been written rather awkwardly on pink writing paper.

Dere Hogfather,

For Hogswatch I would like a drum an a dolly an a teddybear an a Gharstley Omnian Inquisision Torchure Chamber with Wind-up Rack and Nearly Real Blud You Can Use Again. I have been good. I hop the Chimney is big enough but my friend Willaim Says you are my father really.

Yrs. Virginia Prood

The Death of Rats nibbles a bit of the pork pie left out for the Hogfather.

He also raises a leg over one of the turnips as though having a piddle, even though nothing comes out, and then we hear a scraping noise. The Death of Rats looks over to the fireplace.

A few lumps of soot thump into the grate. The scraping becomes louder, is followed by a moment of silence and then a clang as something lands in the ashes and knocks over a set of ornamental fire-irons.

The Death of Rats jumps down from the table onto a bare branch of oak that

56

stands in a pot by the table and watches carefully as a RED-ROBED FIGURE pulls itself upright and staggers across the hearthrug, rubbing its shin where it has been caught by the toasting fork.

It reaches the table and reads the note. There is a groan.

The turnips and the pork pie are pocketed.

The figure scans the dripping note for a moment, and then turns around and approaches the mantelpiece.

The Death of Rats pulls back slightly behind a glass ball and is given a fright as he turns and peers at his hugely distorted reflection.

A red-gloved hand takes down a stocking. There is some creaking and rustling and it is replaced, looking a lot fatter - the larger box sticking out of the top has, just visible, the words:

Victim Figures Not Included. 3-10 yrs.

The figure stands back and pulls a list out of its pocket. It holds it up to the hood and appears to be consulting it. The hood hides all the face of the figure in red, apart from a long white beard. It waves its other hand vaguely at the fireplace, the sooty footprints, the empty sherry glass and the stocking. Then it bends forward, as if reading some tiny print.

                    VOICE
        AH, YES . . . ER . . . HO. HO. HO.

With that, it ducks down and enters the chimney. There is some scrabbling before its boots gain a purchase, and then it is gone.

The Death of Rats on the mantelpiece is gnawing his little scythe's handle in sheer shock.

                    DEATH OF RATS
        SQUEAK.

EXT. VIRGINIA PROOD'S HOUSE/ROOF - NIGHT

The Death of Rats emerges so fast from the chimney that he shoots out with his legs still scrabbling and lands in the snow on the roof where he rolls like a snowball landing in the gutter where . . . there is a sleigh hovering.

                    VOICE IN RED HOOD
        HERE'S ANOTHER PORK PIE.

                    VOICE BEHIND SACKS
        Any mustard? They're a treat with
        mustard.

The red-hooded figure turns back. It is DEATH dressed
as the Hogfather.

                    DEATH OF RATS
        SQUEAK?

DEATH picks up the reins.

                    DEATH
        APPLE! SAUCE!

            The pigs' legs blur. Silver light flicks
            across them, and explodes outwards.
            They dwindle to a dot, and vanish.
            The sleigh is gone.

            The Grim Squeaker watches him go.

                    DEATH OF RATS
        SQUEAK? SQUEAK SQUEAK
        SQUEAK!

        SUBTITLE: Strictly speaking,
        that's not part of the job
        description.

EXT. SKY - NIGHT

            The sleigh soars onwards through
            time and space. DEATH looks
            over his shoulder at the
            sacks.

            They all appear to have
            sticking out of the top a
            teddy bear, a toy soldier, a
            drum and a red-and-white
            candy cane.

                    DEATH
        I'M FINDING THE
        BEARD A BIT OF A
        TRIAL.

> VOICE BEHIND SACKS
> Well, at least it's keeping you in the
> right frame of mind, master. In
> character, sort of thing.

> DEATH
> BUT GOING DOWN THE CHIMNEY? WHERE'S THE
> SENSE IN THAT?

A head thrusts itself out from the pile. It appears to
belong to the oldest, most unpleasant pixie in the
universe. The fact that it is underneath a jolly little
green hat with a bell on it does nothing to improve
matters. It is ALBERT . . . in an ill-fitting Pixie
costume.

> ALBERT
> It's got to be chimneys. Same
> as the beard, really.

He waves a crabbed hand containing a
thick wad of letters, many of them on
pastel-coloured paper.

> ALBERT
> You reckon these little
> buggers'd be writing to
> someone who walked through
> walls? And the 'Ho, ho, ho'
> could use some more work, if
> you don't mind my saying so.

> DEATH
> HO. HO. HO.

> ALBERT
> No, no, no! You got to put
> a bit of life in it, sir,
> no offence intended. It's
> got to be a big fat laugh.
> You got to . . . you got
> to sound like you're
> pissing brandy and crapping
> plum pudding, sir, excuse
> my Klatchian.

Albert pulls out a packet of
CIGARETTE PAPERS and starts to
make a roll-up.

> DEATH
> REALLY? HOW DO YOU KNOW ALL THIS?

                              ALBERT
                    I was young once, sir.

Albert opens a pink sack. It seems to be nearly all
horses. Most of them are grinning. Just as he reaches
for his TOBACCO POUCH in his coat, the wind blows the
paper away.

INT. TOOTH FAIRY'S CASTLE/FOOT OF TOWER – DAY

Chickenwire empties a sack of teeth into the beginnings
of a pile. He sidles towards Medium Dave.

                         CHICKENWIRE
                    These teeth give me the creeps.

                         MEDIUM DAVE
                    Just keep going. The quicker all the
                    teeth are in the pile the quicker we're
                    out of here with our money.

                         CHICKENWIRE
                    Mind you, he's more creepy than the
                    teeth.

They are silent in thought for a moment.

                         MEDIUM DAVE
                    No one ever laid a punch on Banjo since
                    our mam died.

                         CHICKENWIRE
                    Tough but fair, your Ma. I recall that
                    time she strangled Glossy Ron with his
                    own leg.

                         MEDIUM DAVE
                    Yeah.

Chickenwire sweeps some stray teeth into the pile.

                         CHICKENWIRE
                    Maybe the both of us could creep up on
                    him and . . .

                         MEDIUM DAVE
                       (sarcastically)
                    Yeah.

Chickenwire realises that this was probably not a good
idea.

                    CHICKENWIRE
     I keep thinking of that glass eye
     watching me. I keep thinking it can see
     right in my head.

                    MEDIUM DAVE
     Don't worry, he doesn't know what
     you're thinking.

                    CHICKENWIRE
     How d'you know?

                    MEDIUM DAVE
     You're still alive, yeah?

They both look over their shoulders at the same time.

INT. GAITER'S HOUSE/HALL - NIGHT

Susan heads to the schoolroom.

INT. GAITER'S HOUSE/SCHOOL ROOM - NIGHT

Inside, something has changed . . .

Susan glares at the stockings, but they are still
unfilled.

She looks across to the window which is half open . . .

                    SUSAN
     Oh no.

She hears a clicking noise behind her and then a voice comes from the shelves on the other side of the room.

                    RAVEN (O.C.)
          These damn eyeballs are hard, aren't
          they?

                    SUSAN
          They're walnuts, not eyeballs.

The walnuts bounce around her on the floor.

Susan turns, races across the room. The Raven flies off the shelf and out of the window. Susan slams it shut behind him.

The Raven taps at the window pane.

                    SUSAN
          I don't want you back in my life,
          understand?

The Raven keeps tapping on the glass.

But the muffled sound draws Susan closer to listen for a moment.

                    SUSAN
          Warned?

EXT. JAMES RIDDLE'S ROOF - NIGHT

The pigs and sleigh are on the roof. DEATH steps out of the chimney. Albert is waiting in the sleigh.

                    ALBERT
          Did you check the list?

Albert gives a last lick to a ROLL-UP and puts it in his mouth. He starts to look for a light.

                    DEATH
          COULDN'T REALLY MAKE HEAD NOR
          TAIL OF IT, TO TELL YOU THE
          TRUTH. I DON'T NORMALLY CARE IF
          THEY'VE BEEN NAUGHTY OR NICE, FOR
          EXAMPLE.

DEATH gives Albert a pork pie which he carefully examines.

62

                    DEATH
I CAN FEEL THE BELIEF FADING.

                    ALBERT
What's that?

                    DEATH
IT LOOKS VERY BAD.

                    ALBERT
Nah, 's just where something's nibbled
i—

Albert licks his fingers and bites into the pork pie.

                    DEATH
I MEAN THE SITUATION. I FEAR WE MAY BE
TOO LATE.

                    ALBERT
  (with mouth full)
Never say die, master. That's our
motto, eh?

                    DEATH
I CAN'T SAY IT'S EVER REALLY BEEN MINE.

And with that DEATH tugs on the reins and the sleigh
flies away.

INT. GAITER'S HOUSE/SCHOOL ROOM - NIGHT

Susan is still for a moment. She looks over to the
ticking clock. The PENDULUM STOPS MOVING and FREEZES
mid-swing.

Then, suddenly . . .

 . . . there is a scrabbling sound far overhead.

A few flakes of soot drop down the chimney.

Susan glances up at the clock again. It is just on half
past six.

There is a tapping on the window again. Susan turns.

                    RAVEN (O.C.)
You'd better watch out . . .

And with a flutter of wings he is gone.

INT. TOOTH FAIRY'S CASTLE/FOOT OF TOWER - DAY

Teatime is with Sideney by the start of a pile of teeth.

> TEATIME
> . . . Because if the Hogfather still comes to town as a result of a magical misjudgment on your part then you will no longer be my friend, Mr Sideney.

The wizard is holding a piece of chalk. He licks the tip in an attempt to look professional.

> MR SIDENEY
> I understand, sir.

> TEATIME
> Do you have a lot of friends, Mr Sideney?

> MR SIDENEY
> A few, yes.

> TEATIME
> (apologetically)
> I don't have many. Don't seem to have the knack. On the other hand . . . I don't seem to have any enemies at all. Not one. Isn't that nice?

> MR SIDENEY
> (shaking)
> It's a . . . very enemy-friendly spell, sir.

Teatime stares right into Mr Sideney's face.

> MR SIDENEY
> That is . . . very simple.

His discomfort is only broken when we hear a voice shouting from high up in the tower.

> MR BROWN (O.C.)
> Mr Teh-a-time-eh.

Teatime looks up.

At the release of tension in Sideney's fingers he snaps
the chalk.

INT. GAITER'S HOUSE/SCHOOL ROOM - NIGHT

DEATH is stood in the middle of the nursery carpet. The
pillow under Death's red robe slips gently down.

                    SUSAN
        Grandfather . . . !

She walks around him.

                    SUSAN
        This is Hogswatch! It's supposed to be
        jolly, with mistletoe and holly, and -
        and other things ending in olly! It's a
        time when people want to feel good
        about things and eat until they
        explode! It's a time when they want to
        see all their relatives . . .

She stops mid-sentence.

                              SUSAN
               I mean it's a time when humans are
               really human, and they don't want a . . .
               a skeleton at the feast! Especially
               one, I might add, who's wearing a false
               beard and has got a damn cushion shoved
               up his robe! I mean, why?

Susan pulls the pillow out from under his cloak.

DEATH looks nervous.

                              DEATH
               ALBERT SAID IT WOULD HELP ME GET INTO
               THE SPIRIT OF THE THING.

Susan looks over at the sounds of struggling from the
chimney. Susan turns back to DEATH. He is tucking his
artificial Hogfather stomach back in.

                              SUSAN
               This is a real job. And I was looking
               forward to a real Hogswatch, where
               normal things happen with normal people
               in a normal house! And suddenly the old
               circus comes to town. Well, I don't
               know what's going on, but you can all
               leave, right now!

There is a muffled curse, a rush of soot, and Albert
lands in the grate.

                              ALBERT
               Buggr'it!

                              SUSAN
               Albert . . . the pixie?! Come along in,
               do. If the real Hogfather doesn't come
               soon there's not going to be room for
               him.

                              DEATH
               HE WON'T BE JOINING US.

The pillow slides softly onto the rug.

                              SUSAN
               So what have you turned up for? And if
               it's for business reasons, I will add,
               then that outfit is in extremely poor
               taste . . .

                         DEATH
THE HOGFATHER IS . . . UNAVAILABLE.

                         SUSAN
Unavailable? At Hogswatch?

                         DEATH
YES.

                         SUSAN
Why?

                         DEATH
HE IS . . . LET ME SEE . . . THERE
ISN'T AN ENTIRELY APPROPRIATE HUMAN
WORD, SO . . . LET'S SETTLE FOR . . .
GONE. YES. HE IS GONE.

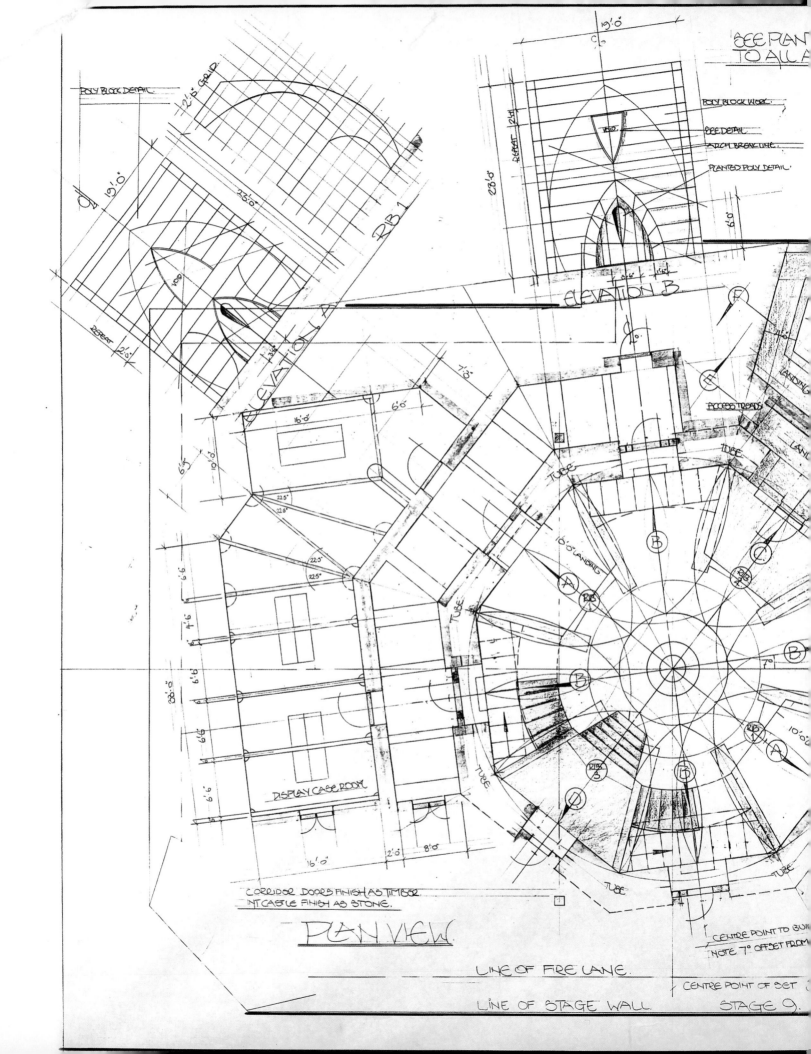

PLAN VIEW

CORRIDOR DOORS FINISH AS TIMBER.
INT CASTLE FINISH AS STONE.

LINE OF FIRE LANE.

LINE OF STAGE WALL.

STAGE 9.

DISPLAY CASE ROOM

POLY BLOCK DETAIL

ELEVATION B

ELEVATION A

POLY BLOCK WORK
SEE DETAIL
ARCH BREAK LINE
PLANTED POLY DETAIL

SEE PLAN
TO ALL

RB 1

VOID

VOID

TUBE

TUBE

TUBE

TUBE

TUBE

ACCESS TREADS

LANDING

10'0" LANDING

CENTRE POINT TO BUILD
NOTE 7° OFFSET FROM
CENTRE POINT OF SET

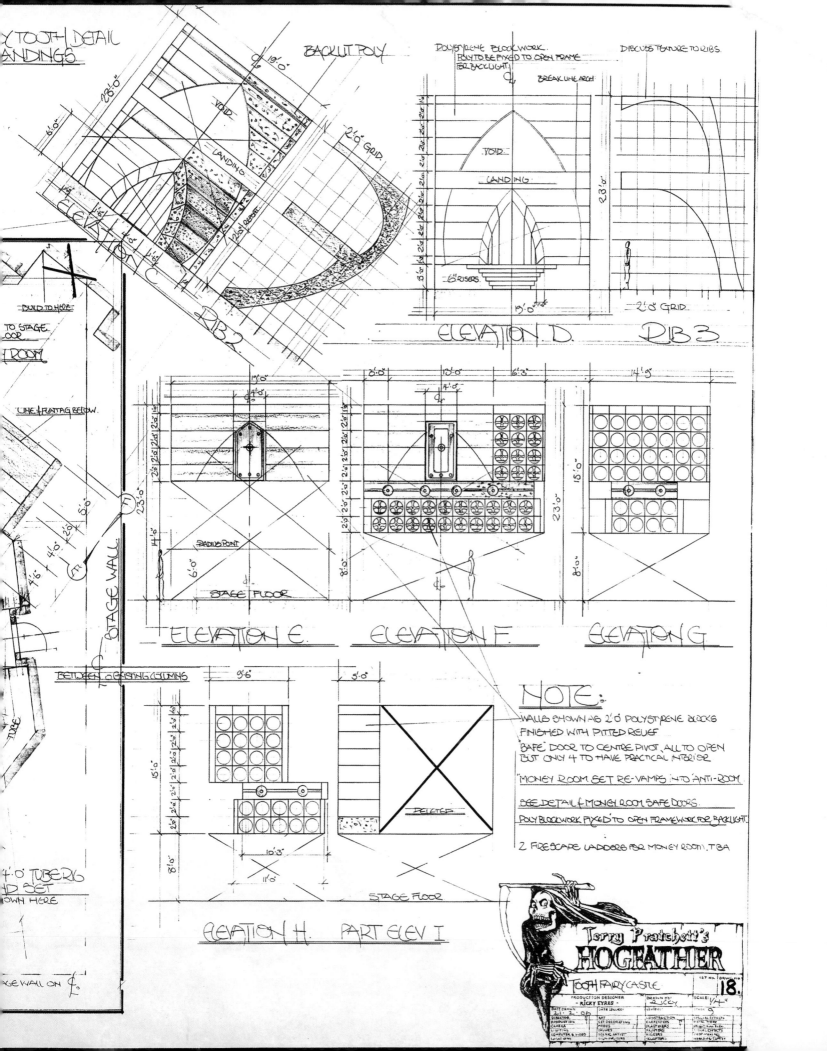

TOOTH DETAIL
LANDINGS

BACKLIT POLY

ELEVATION C   RIB 2

POLYSTYRENE BLOCKWORK.
POLY TO BE FIXED TO OPEN FRAME
FOR BACKLIGHT.

DISCUSS TEXTURE TO RIBS.

BREAK LINE ARCH

VOID

LANDING

6" RISERS

ELEVATION D.   RIB 3

2'0" GRID.

VOID

LANDING

BUILD TO HERE

TO STAGE
DOOR

ROOM

LINE + FLATTAG BELOW

RADIUS POINT

STAGE FLOOR

ELEVATION E.   ELEVATION F.   ELEVATION G

BETWEEN EXISTING COLUMNS

DELETED

STAGE FLOOR

ELEVATION H.   PART ELEV I

NOTE:

WALLS SHOWN AS 2'0" POLYSTYRENE BLOCKS
FINISHED WITH PITTED RELIEF

SAFE DOOR TO CENTRE PIVOT, ALL TO OPEN
BUT ONLY 4 TO HAVE PRACTICAL INTERIOR

'MONEY ROOM' SET RE-VAMPS INTO 'ANTI-ROOM'

SEE DETAIL + MONEY ROOM SAFE DOORS.

POLY BLOCKWORK FIXED TO OPEN FRAMEWORK FOR BACKLIGHT.

2 FIRESCAPE LADDERS FOR MONEY ROOM. TBA

STAGE WALL

Terry Pratchett's
HOGFATHER

TOOTH FAIRY CASTLE

KEY NO. DRAWING NO.
18.

PRODUCTION DESIGNER
- RICKY EYRES -

DRAWN BY
RICKY

SCALE 1/4"

DATE DRAWN
21.2.96

INT. TOOTH FAIRY'S CASTLE/STAIRCASE - DAY

Teatime strides up the stairs to find Mr Brown picking a lock. The last tumbler turns and he steps back.

> MR BROWN
> (grumpy)
> There are a lot of doors. I hope this is the one.

Teatime sniffs the air, then slowly turns the handle and enters the room silently.

INT. TOOTH FAIRY'S CASTLE/DISPLAY CASE ROOM 2 - DAY

Teatime takes one step into doorway and stops. He surveys the room and looks disappointed.

> TEATIME
> Just teeth in here. Keep going, Mr Brown.

Then in a flash he turns behind the door.

> TEATIME
> Boo!

The guard cowering behind it jumps out of his skin. Terror spreads across his face.

INT. TOOTH FAIRY'S CASTLE/FOOT OF TOWER - DAY

The dead guard falls, SMASH, directly into the CAMERA.

EXT. UNSEEN UNIVERSITY/ROOF - NIGHT

The snow-covered rooftops of Ankh-Morpork stretch off into the distance until suddenly . . . right in front of CAMERA . . . THUD. A figure falls right into the foreground. The distinctly DEAD-LOOKING BODY makes an almost perfect GUARD-SHAPED outline in the thick snow.

The CAMERA tracks towards a small gable window. Just in front of it a large TUBE emerges from the roof. It begins to vibrate . . .

                    PONDER STIBBONS (O.C.)
          . . . and radiation shielding.

INT. UNSEEN UNIVERSITY/HEX'S ROOM - NIGHT

  . . . PONDER STIBBONS, a young bespectacled student wizard turns from the keyboard of HEX, a large Heath Robinson THINKING ENGINE.

The University BURSAR is standing nervously by.

                    BURSAR
          You want radiation
          shielding, Mr Stibbons?

He is studying a blackboard with a detailed drawing of what looks like a chemistry set into which a large metal tube runs and then continues right around in a huge loop.

                    PONDER STIBBONS
          Advice from Hex, Bursar.

The Bursar looks at the thinking engine.

                    PONDER STIBBONS
          As the University won't supply us
          students with a thaumic particle
          accelerator, we're starting to build
          our own.

The Bursar looks at a group of student wizards gathered around the beginnings of the accelerator. Sparks fly around a beaker of volatile-looking liquid.

                    PONDER STIBBONS
          Safety first and all that.

The Bursar leaves the room in a hurry.

The accelerator sparks up.

Air pumps into its bellows and the big pipe starts to vibrate dangerously.

INT. UNSEEN UNIVERSITY/GREAT HALL - NIGHT

The Unseen University's Great Hall has been set for the Hogswatchnight Feast. Tables are already groaning under the weight of the cutlery. It is hard to see where any food will fit among the drifts of ornamental fruit bowls and forests of wine glasses.

The Bursar hurries in.

> BURSAR
> Dean, have you seen the Head of Inadvisedly Applied Magic? I need some urgent advice.

The DEAN turns.

> THE DEAN
> Ask the Chair of Indefinite Studies.

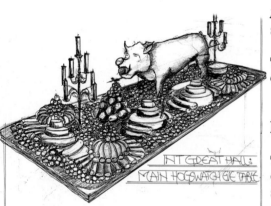

As the CHAIR OF INDEFINITE STUDIES looks round and shrugs indefinitely, we hear a distant explosion.

The glasses and cutlery shake as if in a small earthquake.

EXT. UNSEEN UNIVERSITY/ROOF - NIGHT

There is a secondary thud. Smoke billows from the gable window next to which . . . the distinctively shaped HELMET of the TOOTH FAIRY CASTLE GUARDS tips off its late owner's head and slowly rolls down the roof . . .

INT. UNSEEN UNIVERSITY/GREAT HALL - NIGHT

MUSTRUM RIDCULLY, the ARCHANCELLOR of the Unseen University, wearing his dressing gown and carrying a WASH BAG enters the Hall. His voice booms.

> RIDCULLY
> (to himself)
> I don't know. In my day when I was an undergraduate I wouldn't have been studying on Hogswatchnight. It's just not natural. I'd have been sick twice by now . . .

72

EXT. UNSEEN UNIVERSITY/ROOF – NIGHT

STUDENTS fight for space to retch out of the gable
window as the smoke billows round them.

INT. UNSEEN UNIVERSITY/GREAT HALL – NIGHT

Ridcully turns his back from listening to the distant
sound of coughing and vomiting.

> RIDCULLY
> That's more like it!

He turns his back to the hall, which seems rather
empty. The wizards are all emerging from beneath
various tables.

> RIDCULLY
> Dean, Bursar, Lecturer in Recent Runes,
> how are the Hogswatch banquet
> preparations coming along?

The wizards all turn.

> THE DEAN
> Excellent, though I'm not sure if
> there'll be room for any food on the
> tables.

> RIDCULLY
> Good, well I'm off to spruce up so I've
> decided that as a Hogswatch present to
> myself I'm going to open up the late
> Archchancellor Weatherwax's old
> bathroom so I don't have to sluice
> down with you fellows. It's
> unhygienic. You can catch stuff.

The senior wizards of Unseen University look worried.

INT. UNSEEN UNIVERSITY/ARCHCHANCELLOR'S BATHROOM – NIGHT

The wizards stand and look at the door. Planks have
been nailed right across. A sign hangs from the door
reading DO NOT, UNDER ANY CIRCUMSTANCES, OPEN THIS
DOOR.

> LECTURER IN RECENT RUNES
> Really, Mustrum, I think this is most
> unwise.

Ridcully flourishes his scrubbing brush.

> RIDCULLY
> It says on the plans that it was a
> bathroom. You are all acting as if it's
> some kind of a torture chamber.

> THE DEAN
> A bathroom, designed by Bloody Stupid
> Johnson.

There is a pause. Even Ridcully has to adjust his mind
around this.

> LECTURER IN RECENT RUNES
> The late Bergholt Stuttley Johnson was
> the worst inventor in the world.

> RIDCULLY
> Yes, but not everything he made had a
> horribly fatal flaw. Look at that thing
> they use down in the kitchens for
> peelin' the potatoes, for example.

> LECTURER IN RECENT RUNES
> Ah, you mean the thing with the brass
> plate on it saying 'Improved Manicure
> Device', Archchancellor?

Ridcully opens a fresh bar of soap.

> RIDCULLY
> Listen, it's just water. Even Johnson
> couldn't do much harm with water.

Maybe he has a point.

He gestures to MODO, the University's gardener and odd-
job DWARF, who stands by with a crowbar.

> RIDCULLY
> Go to it, lad.

The gardener salutes and raises the tool. There is the
sound of splintering wood.

INT. TOOTH FAIRY'S CASTLE/DISPLAY CASE ROOM 1 – DAY

A CROWBAR levers open a lid.

Medium Dave's big hand scoops teeth into a sack.

At the opposite end of the room, ranging back to the
distant Dave, are long lines of smashed glass cases.
There are little piles of teeth beneath each one. There
are also cards scattered everywhere.

On one card: the writing is in a meticulous rounded
script. It reads: *Thomas Ague, aged 4 and nearly three-quarters, 9 Castle
View, Sto Lat.*

A solitary TOOTH falls in slow motion and bounces onto
the stone floor next to the card until it stops dead
. . . still.

INT. GAITER'S HOUSE/SCHOOL ROOM - NIGHT

DEATH looks down at Susan with a pained expression.

Susan is pacing in front of him.

> SUSAN
> How can the Hogfather be gone?
> He's . . . isn't he what you
> are? An . . .

> DEATH

> ANTHROPOMORPHIC
> PERSONIFICATION. YES. HE HAS
> BECOME SO THE SPIRIT OF
> HOGSWATCH.

> SUSAN
> (ignoring him)
> And while he's gone you've
> taken over? That's sick!

Albert brushes past her and opens the
door. Susan pushes it shut quickly.

DEATH leans down. Susan stares up into the blue glow of
his eyes.

A couple of letters appear in DEATH's hand.

> DEATH
> I SEE THE GIRL WRITES IN GREEN CRAYON
> ON PINK PAPER WITH A MOUSE IN THE
> CORNER. THE MOUSE IS WEARING A DRESS.

> SUSAN
> I ought to point out that she decided
> to do that so the Hogfather would think

she was sweet. Including the deliberate
bad spelling. But look, why are you ...

                    DEATH
SHE SAYS SHE IS FIVE YEARS OLD.

                    SUSAN
In years, yes. In cynicism, she's about
thirty-five. Why are you doing the . . . ?

                    DEATH
BUT SHE BELIEVES IN THE HOGFATHER?

                    SUSAN
She'd believe in anything if there was
a dolly in it for her. But you're not
going to leave without telling me . . .

DEATH hangs the stockings back on the mantelpiece.

Susan turns to Albert who has spotted the glass of
sherry and couple of turnips that the children have
left on the table and is bearing down on them.

                    SUSAN
And what are you doing here, Albert? I
thought you'd die if you ever came back
to the world!

                    DEATH
AH, BUT WE ARE NOT IN THE WORLD. WE
ARE IN THE SPECIAL CONGRUENT REALITY
CREATED FOR THE HOGFATHER. NORMAL
RULES HAVE TO BE SUSPENDED. HOW ELSE
COULD ANYONE GET AROUND THE ENTIRE
WORLD IN ONE NIGHT?

                    ALBERT
        (leering)
's right. One of the Hogfather's
Little Helpers, me. Official. Got
the pointy green hat and everything.

Albert spits into the fireplace.

                    ALBERT
Been good, 'ave yer?

Susan stares at him.

                    DEATH
NOW WE MUST BE GOING. HAPPY
HOGSWATCH. ER . . . OH, YES:

Susan is about to speak again.

                    DEATH
        HO. HO. HO.

Albert wipes his mouth.

                    ALBERT
        Nice sherry.

Rage overtakes Susan's curiosity.

                    SUSAN
        You've actually been drinking the
        actual drinks little children leave out
        for the actual Hogfather?

                    ALBERT
        Yeah, why not? He ain't drinking 'em.
        Not where he's gone.

                    SUSAN
        And how many have you had, may I ask?

                    ALBERT
          (Happily)
        Dunno, ain't counted.

                    DEATH
        ONE MILLION, EIGHT HUNDRED THOUSAND,
        SEVEN HUNDRED AND SIX. AND SIXTY-EIGHT
        THOUSAND, THREE HUNDRED AND NINETEEN
        PORK PIES. AND ONE TURNIP.

                    ALBERT
        It looked pork-pie-shaped. Everything
        does, after a while.

                    SUSAN
          (screaming)
        Why are you doing this?

                    DEATH
        I AM SORRY. I CANNOT TELL YOU. FORGET
        YOU SAW ME. IT'S NOT YOUR BUSINESS.

                    SUSAN
        Not my business? How can—

                    DEATH
        YOU WANTED TO BE NORMAL. GOOD NIGHT . . .
        GRANDDAUGHTER . . .

ALBERT

    Sleepy tight.

Albert belches.

ALBERT

    I shall.

The clock strikes, twice, for the half-hour. It is still half past six but the PENDULUM starts swinging again.

And they are gone.

In Twyla's pink stocking on the mantelpiece is a DOLLY.

INT. UNSEEN UNIVERSITY/ARCHCHANCELLOR'S BATHROOM – NIGHT

Mustrum Ridcully is sat in a chair wearing a dressing gown.

RIDCULLY
How are we doing Mr Modo?

Modo salutes.

MODO

    The tanks are full and I've stoked the boilers, Mr Archchancellor, Sir.

Ridcully gets up and walks down the corridor.

THE DEAN
You did read the sign on the door, Ridcully?

Ridcully ignores him.

BURSAR
The sign which said do not under any circumstances open the door.

RIDCULLY
Oh, they just wrote that to keep people out.

THE DEAN
Don't say I didn't warn you.

>   RIDCULLY
> Hygiene, that's the ticket.

>   MODO
> I still haven't worked out
> where all the pipes lead.

>   RIDCULLY
>   (Happily)
> We'll find out. Never you
> fear!

The room is a sanitary poem in
mahogany, rosewood and copper. Every
pipe and brass tap has been polished
until they gleam.

Ridcully removes his hat and puts on
a shower cap of his own design. In
deference to his profession, it's
pointy. He picks up a yellow rubber duck.

>   RIDCULLY
> Man the pumps, Mr Modo. Or dwarf them,
> of course, in your case.

>   MODO
> Yes, Archchancellor.

Modo hauls on a lever. The pipes start a hammering
noise and steam leaks out of a few joints.

The rest of the wizards back away.

Ridcully shuts the frosted door of the Ablutorium
behind him, his face beaming with expectation.

INT. CHILD'S BEDROOM/ANKH-MORPORK - NIGHT

DEATH fills a stocking. Albert preps a roll-up.

>   ALBERT
> Susan'll try to find out what this is
> all about, you know.

>   DEATH
> OH DEAR.

>   ALBERT
> Especially after you told her not to.

>   DEATH
> YOU THINK SO?

                    ALBERT
     Yep.

Albert carefully drops tobacco into a cigarette paper.

                    DEATH
          DEAR ME. I STILL HAVE A LOT TO LEARN
          ABOUT HUMANS, DON'T I?

                    ALBERT
     Oh . . . I dunno . . .

                    DEATH
          OBVIOUSLY IT WOULD BE QUITE WRONG TO
          INVOLVE A HUMAN IN ALL THIS. THAT IS
          WHY, YOU WILL RECALL, I CLEARLY FORBADE
          HER TO TAKE AN INTEREST.

                    ALBERT
     Yep . . . you did . . .

Albert starts to delicately fold the cigarette.

                    DEATH
          BESIDES, IT'S AGAINST THE RULES.

                    ALBERT
     Shame she's used to breaking 'em
     really.

                    DEATH
          YOU MIGHT THINK I'VE ALREADY THOUGHT OF
          THAT BUT I COULDN'T POSSIBLY COMMENT.

DEATH stares ahead for a moment and then shrugs.

                    DEATH
          AND WE HAVE SO MUCH TO DO. WE HAVE THE
          HOGFATHER'S PROMISES TO KEEP.

Albert bends down to look up the chimney flue and the
draft blows his tobacco up the chimney.

INT. ARCHCHANCELLOR'S BATHROOM/ABLUTORIUM - NIGHT

Ridcully sings loudly.

                    RIDCULLY
     Mi, mi, mi!

                        80

The Archchancellor's voice reverberates back at him and he smiles as he sees a tap marked 'Old Faithful'. He leans over and opens it. He starts to sing again.

INT. ARCHCHANCELLOR'S BATHROOM – NIGHT

Ridcully's voice booms out through the thick clouds of steam until . . . the song rises to a falsetto and stops abruptly. All Modo can hear is a ferocious gushing noise.

>   MODO
>   Archchancellor?

Modo spins a wheel. The gushing sound gradually subsides. Moments later he pushes open the door and helps a rather pale Ridcully out and onto a bench.

>   RIDCULLY
>   (high-pitched voice)
>   There's a tap in there marked 'Old
>   Faithful' . . .

Ridcully coughs.

>   RIDCULLY
>   (low normal voice)
>   . . . which we perhaps should leave
>   alone for now.

INT. GAITER'S HOUSE/SCHOOL ROOM – NIGHT

Susan stands by the fireplace looking at the dolly in Twyla's stocking, thinking.

>   SUSAN
>   Has he done something to the real
>   Hogfather?

She looks out into the middle distance, thinking.

INT. GAITER'S HOUSE/TWYLA'S BEDROOM – NIGHT

Susan quietly opens the door to the bedroom.

Twyla and Gawain are sound asleep.

Susan watches them for a moment and then goes over and kisses them gently.

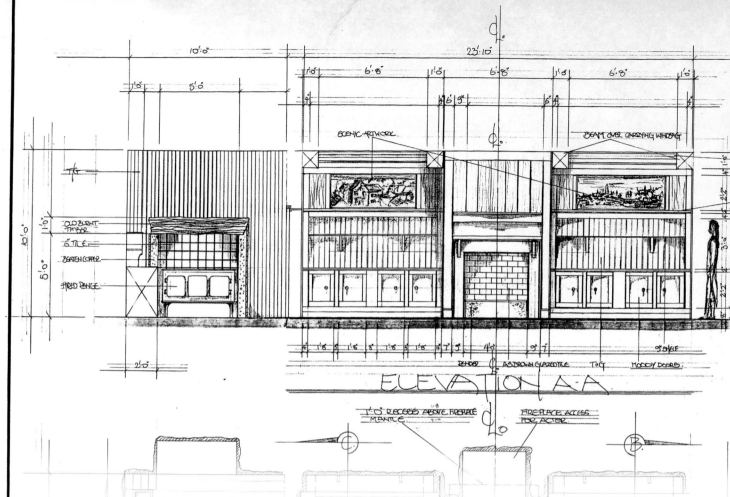

ELEVATION A-A

She stands up. From the back of her head the HAIR
starts to MORPH from its prim governess style into
freaky GOTH MODE until we reveal a look of steely
resolve on Susan's face.

She shuts her eyes and CLICKS her fingers. When they
open she hears the clock stop ticking. The last tick is
long-drawn-out, like a death rattle.

Time stops. But duration continues.

And she is gone.

INT. GAITER'S HOUSE/BACK STAIRS - NIGHT

Susan hurries down the stairs and lets herself out of
the front door.

EXT. GAITER'S HOUSE - NIGHT

Snow hangs motionless in the air. It sparkles
electronically as she walks through it.

There is traffic in the street, but it is fossilised in Time. The flakes gather on her coat, leaving behind her a Susan-shaped tunnel in the hanging snow.

She reaches the gate to the house where the snow mounds the bushes and trees in pure white.

There is no noise. The curtains of snow shut out the city lights.

EXT. GAITER'S HOUSE/SIDE – NIGHT

Susan sticks her fingers into her mouth and whistles.

Then suddenly there are hoof-beats and the floating snow bursts open and Binky is there. He trots round in a circle, and then stands and steams. Susan looks at him, deciding, for the briefest of moments . . . and then jumps on his back.

Binky and Susan fly off . . .

And as the snow starts to fall again, the Auditors materialise. The snow falls through them as they ruminate.

> AUDITOR 3
> Can she be eliminated?

> AUDITOR 2
> Oh yes.

> AUDITOR 3
> Oh good.

> AUDITOR 4
> Then can we go back to just concentrating on running the universe? Making sure that gravity works and that atoms spin?

> AUDITOR 1
> Yes, when there's not an atom of belief left in the Discworld.

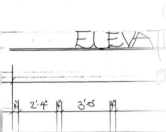

INT. TOOTH FAIRY'S CASTLE/FOOT OF TOWER - NIGHT

Banjo sweeps another brushful of teeth into the large
pile building in the centre of the tower.

EXT. ARCHCHANCELLOR'S BATHROOM - NIGHT

Ridcully slowly and carefully dries his feet on a
big fluffy towel. He leans closer to inspect
between his toes.

> THE DEAN
> What are you looking for, Mustrum?

> RIDCULLY
> My father told me that where you get
> lots of people bathing together, the
> Verruca Gnome is running around with
> his little sack.

He stands and shouts into the
Ablutorium.

> RIDCULLY
> Modo! No sign of the Verruca
> Gnome in there, is there,
> old boy?

INT. UNSEEN UNIVERSITY/ARCHCHANCELLOR'S BATHROOM - NIGHT

Modo wipes his hands on a piece
of rag and looks proudly at his
handiwork. Shining porcelain
gleams back at him.

The floors have been scrubbed to a
gleam.

> MODO
> (to himself)
> Verruca Gnome.

He gives a tap a last polish.

> MODO
> What an imagination the Gentlemen do
> have.

Somewhere in the distance there is a
glingleglingleglingle noise, like little silver bells . . .

EXT. UNSEEN UNIVERSITY/ROOF - NIGHT

. . . and someone lands abruptly in the thick snow.

> VOICE IN SNOW
> Bugger!

. . . and rolls down the pitch of the roof.

The tiny hunched shape slides and slithers along the
gutter through the slush, swearing under its breath
until it drops into a down pipe and disappears from
sight.

EXT. UNSEEN UNIVERSITY/COURTYARD - NIGHT

At the bottom of the drainpipe it shoots out into a
snowdrift.

Moments later it struggles out of the snow. It wears a
stained black suit and, on its head a 'bowler' or
'derby' HAT. The hat is pressed down very firmly so
that as the creature has long pointy ears, these are
forced out sideways and give it the look of a small
malignant wing-nut. Over its shoulder it has a small
CLOTH SACK.

The gnome-like thing goes back to the bottom of the
drainpipe. Without pausing, his swearing becomes
muffled as he starts to climb up the inside of the
pipe.

EXT. DEATH'S HOUSE - NIGHT

DEATH's extensive lawn stretches out in front of the
house, surrounded by extensive areas of topiary. In the
foreground is an ornamental fish pond surrounded by
cheerful little skeletal fishing gnomes.

INT. DEATH'S HOUSE/LIBRARY - NIGHT

DEATH's desk is a mess. Susan looks through the papers,
glancing up but quickly ignoring a FRAMED PICTURE of
herself as a child on DEATH's knee.

                    RAVEN
          You took your time.

Susan turns.

                    SUSAN
          I don't do family reunions.

Books lie open, piled on one another. There is a note
in his non-serifed handwriting. It looks as though he's
been trying to work something out:

MEMO: DON'T FORGET THE SOOTY FOOTPRINTS. MORE PRACTISE
ON THE HO HO HO. CUSHION.

She puts the paper back carefully, pensive.

By the desk stands DEATH's SWORD. Its thin blue blade
pulses.

INT. DEATH'S HOUSE/LIFETIMERS ROOM - NIGHT

Susan looks round briefly at the infinite shelves of
Lifetimers and is about to leave when she notices an
open door. She goes over
to it.

It is disguised. A whole
section of shelving,
complete with its
whispering glasses, has
slid out.

She steps into the
doorway and starts down
the spiral staircase.

INT. DEATH'S HOUSE/LIEFETIMERS SECRET ROOM - NIGHT

The secret smaller room
on the other side is
lined floor to ceiling
with more hourglasses
that Susan can just see
dimly in the light from
the big room. She steps
inside . . .

We have seen these hourglasses before. These are the
ones made of highlights and shadows with no real
substance we saw when DEATH was in this room . . . the
Lifetimers of the Gods, and beneath them, smaller ones
. . .

                    SUSAN
          The Sandman? John Barleycorn? The Soul
          Cake Duck? The Tooth Fairy?

Susan stops.

INT. TOOTH FAIRY'S CASTLE/DISPLAY CASE ROOM 2 - NIGHT

An axe smashes a glass case. A tooth flies and lands
in Chickenwire's hair. Tiny teeth start to cascade
from the opening.

Chickenwire lowers the axe, picks the tooth out of his
hair with revulsion on his face and drops it. As he
starts to move to the next cabinet, one of his feet
lumbers onto the tooth. It crunches loudly as we . . .

                              SMASH CUT TO:

INT. DEATH'S HOUSE/LIEFETIMERS SECRET ROOM - NIGHT

Something crunches under SUSAN's feet.

There are shards of glass on the floor. She reaches
down and picks up the biggest. Only a few letters
remain of the name etched into the glass. HOGFA

                    SUSAN
          Grandfather . . . what have you done?

Susan leaves the room and as she does, the candles
wink out. Darkness springs back. And in the darkness,
among the spilled sand, there is a faint sizzle and a
tiny spark of light . . .

EXT. ROOF TOP - NIGHT

DEATH throws the sack into the back of the sleigh,
climbs in after it and hitches his belt.

DEATH
THIS CUSHION IS STILL UNCOMFORTABLE.

Albert unscrews the top of a bottle of cold tea. He
takes a pull and starts to put the final touches to a
cigarette.

> **ALBERT**
> You're doing well, master.
> All the soot in the
> fireplace, the footprints,
> them swigged sherries, the
> sleigh tracks all over the
> roofs . . . it's got to work.
>
> **DEATH**
> YOU THINK SO?
>
> **ALBERT**
> Here's a tip, though. Just
> 'Ho. Ho. Ho.' will do. Don't
> say, 'Cower, brief mortals'.

DEATH looks down dejectedly to see
the hundreds of snowy roofs without
sleigh tracks ahead of them.

> **DEATH**
> SO MANY CHIMNEYS. IT WOULD
> BE SO MUCH QUICKER IF I
> LOST THE CUSHION.
>
> **ALBERT**
> If we're going to give
> Susan enough time to
> succeed, the little
> perishers need to believe
> in you . . . I mean the
> Hogfather. So you've got to
> look the part, master.

Albert looks down at his notebook
to see the endless list of names.

> **ALBERT**
> Now, what'll really do some good is a
> public appearance.
>
> **DEATH**
> OH. I DON'T NORMALLY DO THEM.

                    ALBERT
The Hogfather's more've a public
figure, master. And one good public
appearance'll do more good than any
amount of letting kids see you by
accident. Good for the old belief
muscles.

                    DEATH
REALLY?

                    ALBERT
And I know just the place.

DEATH thinks for a moment.

                    DEATH
LET'S GO SLEIGH THEM.

And then he pauses.

                    DEATH
I DON'T KNOW IF YOU NOTICED, ALBERT,
BUT THAT WAS A PUNE, OR PLAY ON WORDS.

                    ALBERT
Ho Ho Ho, sir.

Albert flourishes his completed roll-up.

INT. CRUMLEY'S DEPARTMENT STORE - NIGHT

A magnificent GROTTO takes up nearly all of the first
floor of the store. The Hogfather's SLEIGH is a work of
art in itself. It has delicate silver curly bits on it,
every twinkling star carefully glued on. The PIGS look
really real and a wonderful shade of pink.

VERNON CRUMLEY, the store owner, looks proudly on.

And the kiddies are queuing up with their parents and
watching the display owlishly.

Vernon looks across to the middle of the floor.

There is a cashier in a little cage. Staff are taking
money from customers, putting it in a little clockwork
cable car, and sending it whizzing overhead to the
cashier, who makes change and starts it rattling back
again.

Mr Crumley tucks his fingers in the pockets of his waistcoat and beams. Then he looks down at the pile of coins in front of the cashier.

Suddenly . . . a bright little zig-zag crackles off them and earths itself on the metal grille.

Mr Crumley turns to look at the Hogfather display as it . . .

. . . changes . . . or rather, disintegrates and shatters. The four pink papier-mâché pigs explode.

A cardboard snout bounces off Mr Crumley's head.

The sleigh has changed. The splendour of it is lying in glittering shards around a sleigh that looks as though it has been built of crudely sawn tree trunks laid on two massive wooden runners. It looks ancient and there are faces carved on the wood, nasty crude grinning faces that look quite out of place.

And there, sweating and grunting in the place where the little piggies had been, were . . . well, they look like pigs. They are huge, grey and bristly and have pointy ears and rings through their noses, more like . . . HOGS. A cloud of acrid mist hangs over each one.

One of the pigs turns to look at Crumley with small, red eyes.

                    HOG
          Ghnaaaarrrwnnkh?

INT. CRUMLEY'S DEPARTMENT STORE/KIDS DEPT - NIGHT

Parents are yelling and trying to pull their children away from the Hogfather's sleigh, but they aren't having much luck. The children are gravitating towards it like flies to jam.

Mr Crumley runs towards the terrible thing, waving
his hands.

                    VERNON CRUMLEY
          Stop that! Stop that! You'll frighten
          the Kiddies!

But behind him . . .

                    SMALL BOY (O.C.)
          They've got tusks! Cool!

And then we see his sister also glued to the
display.

                    SMALL BOY'S SISTER
          Hey, look, that one's doing a wee!

A tremendous cloud of yellow steam arises from
behind the boar.

Mr Crumley, tears of anger streaming down his
face, fights through the milling crowd until he
reaches the Hogfather's Grotto. He grabs a
frightened PIXIE.

                    VERNON CRUMLEY
             (shouting)
          It's the Campaign for Equal Heights
          that've done this, isn't it! They're
          out to ruin me!

The pixie hesitates. Children are clustering around
the pigs, despite the continued efforts of their
mothers. The small girl is giving one of them an
orange.

A red and white figure pushes its way through the
crush and rams a false beard into Mr Crumley's hands.

                    GROTTO HOGFATHER
          That's it. I don't mind the smell of
          oranges and the damp trousers but I
          ain't putting up with this.

He stamps off through the queue.

                    GROTTO HOGFATHER (O.C.)
          And he's not even doin' it right!

Mr Crumley forces his way onward.

INT. CRUMLEY'S DEPARTMENT STORE/GROTTO - NIGHT

SOMEONE is sitting in the big chair. There is a child on his knee.

Crumley looks concerned and confused.

From Crumley's POV we see that it is definitely in something like a Hogfather costume, but his eye keeps slipping and won't focus. The figure is on the very edge of his vision.

> VERNON CRUMLEY
> What's going on here?

> A hand takes his shoulder firmly. He turns round and looks into the face of a GROTTO PIXIE. It looks as though its costume has been put on somewhat askew and in a hurry.

> VERNON CRUMLEY
> Who are you?

> The pixie puts a cigarette in its mouth and leers at him.

> ALBERT
> Call me Uncle Heavy.

> VERNON CRUMLEY
> You're not a pixie!

> ALBERT
> Nah, I'm a fairy cobbler, mister. Now you just keep quiet.

> Behind Crumley . . .

> DEATH (O.C.)
> AND WHAT DO YOU WANT FOR HOGSWATCH, SMALL HUMAN?

Mr Crumley turns in horror.

INT. DEATH'S HOUSE/LIBRARY - NIGHT

There is a flutter of wings behind Susan as she searches along the shelves in the canyons of DEATH's huge library.

Susan stops.

>   SUSAN
>   (to herself)
>   Why has he killed The Hogfather . . . ?

There are several shelves, not just one book on the
Hogfather. The first volume seems to be written on a
roll of animal skin.

>   RAVEN
>   The autobiographies write
>   down everything that happens
>   to you just as it happens . . .

>   SUSAN
>   I know. I used to live here,
>   remember?

She looks more closely at the book.

>   SUSAN
>   But I can't read this! The
>   letters are all . . . odd . . .

>   RAVEN
>   'n I suppose now you'll be
>   wanting me words of occult
>   wisdom . . .

Susan pauses and then reluctantly nods.

>   RAVEN
>   Ethereal runes. The Hogfather ain't
>   human, after all.

Susan looks up.

>   RAVEN
>   'n I suppose a bit of warm liver's out
>   of the question . . .

INT. ARCHCHANCELLOR'S BATHROOM - NIGHT

The Archchancellor is dressed in a robe, cutting his
toenails. The clippings fall into an envelope.

>   RIDCULLY
>   (singing again)
>   On the second day of Hogswatch I . . .
>   sent my true love back . . . a nasty

little letter, hah, yes indeed, and a
partridge in a pear tree . . .

Ridcully suddenly spins. A corner of wet towel catches
a small creature on the ear and flicks it onto its
back. It's the GNOME in THE BOWLER HAT with the little
sack.

                    RIDCULLY
          What's the game, then? Small-time
          thief, are you?

The gnome slides backwards on the soapy surface.

                    VERRUCA GNOME
          'ere, what's your game, mister, you
          ain't supposed to be able to see me!

                    RIDCULLY
          I'm a wizard! We can see things that
          are really there, you know. What's in
          this bag?

Ridcully looks interested, and starts to undo
 the string.

                    VERRUCA GNOME
               (pleading)
           You'll really wish you hadn't,
          mister!

                    RIDCULLY
          Will I? What're you doing here, young
          man?

           The gnome gives up.

                    VERRUCA GNOME
           You know the Tooth Fairy? Well,
            it's sort of like the same
          business . . .

                    RIDCULLY
          What? You take things away?

                    VERRUCA GNOME
           Er, not take away, as
            such. More sort of . . .
          bring . . .

                    RIDCULLY
          Ah . . . like new teeth?

96

VERRUCA GNOME
Er . . . like new verrucas.

RIDCULLY
Oh. You're him!

Archchancellor Ridcully nods, looks at the sack,
tightens it back up and then thinks again.

INT. CRUMLEY'S DEPARTMENT STORE/GROTTO - NIGHT

In front of the usurping HOGFATHER is a small CHILD
of indeterminate sex who seems to be mostly woollen
bobble hat.

BOBBLE HAT CHILD
(sniggering)
I saw your piggie do a wee!

DEATH
OH. ER . . . GOOD.

BOBBLE HAT CHILD
It had a gwate big . . .

DEATH
(hurriedly)
WHAT DO YOU WANT FOR HOGSWATCH?

BOBBLE HAT CHILD'S MOTHER
She wants a . . .

The HOGFATHER snaps his fingers impatiently.
The MOTHER's mouth slams shut.

The child seems to sense that this is a once-
in-a-lifetime opportunity . . .

BOBBLE HAT CHILD
I wanta narmy. Anna big castle wif
pointy bits and a swored.

Albert nudges the HOGFATHER.

ALBERT
They're supposed to thank you.

DEATH
ARE YOU SURE? PEOPLE DON'T, NORMALLY.

ALBERT
I meant they thank the Hogfather, which

is you, right?

As Albert is just about to light his cigarette, DEATH
glares at him and nods his head towards the child.
Albert hides the fag behind his back.

> DEATH
> YES, OF COURSE. AHM. YOU'RE
> SUPPOSED TO SAY THANK YOU.

> BOBBLE HAT CHILD
> 'nk you.

> DEATH
> AND BE GOOD. THIS IS PART OF
> THE ARRANGEMENT.

> BOBBLE HAT CHILD
> 'es.

> DEATH
> THEN WE HAVE A CONTRACT.

The HOGFATHER reaches into his sack and
produces . . . a very large model
CASTLE with pointy blue cone roofs on
turrets suitable for princesses to be
locked in . . . a box of several
hundred assorted KNIGHTS and . . . a SWORD. It is four
feet long and glints along the blade.

The mother takes a deep breath.

> BOBBLE HAT CHILD'S MOTHER
> (screaming)
> You can't give her that! It's not safe!

> DEATH
> IT'S A SWORD. THEY'RE NOT MEANT TO BE
> SAFE.

> VERNON CRUMLEY
> (shouting)
> She's a child!

> DEATH
> IT'S EDUCATIONAL.

> VERNON CRUMLEY
> What if she cuts herself?

> DEATH
> THAT WILL BE AN IMPORTANT LESSON.

Albert whispers urgently.

                    DEATH
     REALLY? OH, WELL. IT'S NOT FOR ME TO
     ARGUE, I SUPPOSE.

The blade turns wooden.

          BOBBLE HAT CHILD'S MOTHER
     And she doesn't want all that
     other stuff! She's a girl! Anyway,
     I can't afford big posh stuff like
     that!

                    DEATH
     (bewildered)
     I THOUGHT I GAVE IT AWAY.

     BOBBLE HAT CHILD'S MOTHER
     You do?

        VERNON CRUMLEY
     (horrified)
     You do? You don't! That's our
     Merchandise! You can't give it
     away! Hogswatch isn't about giving
     it all away!

He sees that people were watching and . . .

            VERNON CRUMLEY
     I mean . . . yes, of course things are
     given away . . . but first they have
     to be bought, d'you see?

        BOBBLE HAT CHILD'S MOTHER
     You mean this is all free?

Mr Crumley looks helplessly at the toys. Then he tries
to look hard at the new HOGFATHER.

Crumley's POV tells him that this is a
fat jolly man in a red and white suit
. . . or does it?

          VERNON CRUMLEY
     It . . . seems to be . . .

INT. DEATH'S HOUSE/LIBRARY - NIGHT

Susan blinks and thinks.

                    SUSAN
          None of this is right. Everyone knows
          he's just a jolly old fat man who hands
          out presents to kids!

                    RAVEN
          He wasn't always so jolly. You know how
          it is.

                    SUSAN
          Do I?

                    RAVEN
          It's like, you know, industrial re-
          training. Even gods have to move with
          the times.

Susan runs her hands over the thin leather. The . . .
shapes flow around her fingers. She closes her eyes and
smells deeply through her nostrils. Her breath
condenses in the air.

INT. UNSEEN UNIVERSITY/ARCHCHANCELLOR'S BATHROOM – NIGHT

Ridcully lifts the lid of an ornate jar marked BATH
SALTS and pulls out a bottle of wine.

                    RIDCULLY
          Verrucas, eh?

                    VERRUCA GNOME
          Wish I knew why.

He extracts the cork with a pop.

                    RIDCULLY
          You mean you don't know?

                    VERRUCA GNOME
          Nope. Suddenly I wake up and I'm the
          Verruca Gnome.

                    RIDCULLY
          Strange . . .

Ridcully frowns, then shakes his head and points to a
pot supported on the wall by decorative mermaids.

                    RIDCULLY
          Anyway, amazing bathroom, ain't it?
          It's even got a special pot for your

toenail clippings.

> VERRUCA GNOME
> A special pot for nail clippings?

> RIDCULLY
> Oh, can't be too careful. Get hold of
> something like someone's nail
> clippings, hair, teeth and you've got
> 'em under your control. That's real old
> magic. Dawn of time stuff. Powerful!

He takes a swig of wine, thinking hard, and empties the
envelope of his new clippings into the circular pot . . .

> DISSOLVE TO:

INT. TOOTH FAIRY'S CASTLE/FOOT OF TOWER – DAY

. . . the circular pile of teeth from above now towers
over the gang.

Banjo sweeps the very last tooth into the pile.

Teatime, on the stairs high above, smiles.

> TEATIME
> Children of the world . . .
> prepare to
> think as you
> are told.

He gestures to
Sideney.

> TEATIME
> Mr Sideney.
> Your big
> . . . no
> misjudgments,
> magic moment.

Sideney pulls the
small piece of chalk
from behind his ear
and takes a big
breath.

The tiny stub of chalk
in Sideney's fingers
draws a chalk line. It
comes to a stop as it

reaches the end of another chalk line.

INT. DEATH'S HOUSE/LIBRARY - NIGHT

Susan holds the autobiography.

The Raven scratches at his beak.

> RAVEN
> (expansively)
> Yer see, yer Hogfather was probably
> just your basic winter demi-urge. You
> know . . . blood on the snow, making
> the sun come up.

> SUSAN
> There has to be blood to make the sun
> come up?

Susan looks down at the book. On her face as if from
the scroll's POV, we hear sounds: of hooves, the snap
of branches in a freezing forest . . . . blood.

> RAVEN (O.C.)
> Starts off with animal sacrifice,
> y'know, hunt some big hairy animal to
> death, that kind of stuff. Very
> folkloric, very myffic.

And then just above the scroll, translucent images to
match these words and sound appear: Galloping hooves,
snow on branches. Then Robes and Crowns . . .

> RAVEN (O.C.)
> Didn't stop at animals neither. They
> had sacred kings, the strongest and the
> best, died at the dark time of year to
> give life to the unconquered sun. And
> in a way the Hogfather was all of them.

Until finally . . . a bright shining ball . . .

Susan jerks awake and thrusts the scroll aside. The
images are gone. She unrolls the next scroll, which
looks as though it is made of strips of bark.

> SUSAN
> And then?

She closes her eyes. Characters hover over the surface
of the scroll like a Braille for the touching mind.

                    RAVEN (O.C.)
          (very fast)
     Then some bright spark thought, hey,
     looks like that damn sun comes up
     anyway, so how come we're giving those
     druids all this free grub? The world
     moves on and he's got to find a new
     job.

Images ribbon above the book: wet fur, sweat, pine,
soot, iced air, pig . . . manure. There is blood . . .

                    SUSAN
     So he started as an animal sacrifice to
     make the sun come up, and now he gives
     out presents.

                    RAVEN
     Exactimundo!

Susan looks up, thinking.

INT. CRUMLEY'S DEPARTMENT STORE - NIGHT

Mr Crumley sits on the damp stairs and sobs.

                VOICE OF NOBBS (O.C.)
     Top of the evenin', squire.

He looks up blearily at the small yet irregularly
uniformed figure that has addressed him thusly.

                CORPORAL NOBBS
     I am Corporal Nobbs of the Watch. And
     this is Constable Visit, sir.

CORPORAL NOBBS points to his colleague, CONSTABLE
VISIT, a thin neatly turned out member of the WATCH. He
is exotic-looking. Nobby tears off a salute. Crumley
stands up and waves a shaking finger towards the top of
the stairs.

                VERNON CRUMLEY
     I want you to arrest him!

                CORPORAL NOBBS
     Arrest who, sir?

                VERNON CRUMLEY
     The Hogfather!

                        104

CORPORAL NOBBS
What for, sir?

VERNON CRUMLEY
Because he's sitting up there as bold
as brass in his Grotto, giving away
presents!

CORPORAL NOBBS
Not quite up to speed here, sir. I
thought the Hogfather is supposed to
give away stuff. Isn't he?

VERNON CRUMLEY
This is an impostor!

                    CORPORAL NOBBS
Y'know, I always thought that. I
thought, every year, the Hogfather
spends a fortnight sitting in a wooden
grotto in a shop in Ankh-Morpork? At
his busy time, too? That's not likely.

                    VERNON CRUMLEY
I meant . . . he's not the Hogfather
we usually have.

                    CORPORAL NOBBS
Oh, a different Hogfather? Not the real
impostor at all.

                    VERNON CRUMLEY
Well . . . Yes . . . No . . .

Corporal Nobbs is confused.

                    CORPORAL NOBBS
Arrest the Hogfather, style of thing?

                    VERNON CRUMLEY
Yes!

                    CONSTABLE VISIT
On Hogswatchnight?

                    VERNON CRUMLEY
Yes!

                    CONSTABLE VISIT
For giving away presents?

                    VERNON CRUMLEY
Yes!

                    CORPORAL NOBBS
In front of all those kiddies?

                    VERNON CRUMLEY
Ye . . .

                    CORPORAL NOBBS
In your shop?

                    VERNON CRUMLEY
Yes, do you think it might look a bit
bad?

                    CORPORAL NOBBS
          Hard to see how it could look good
          really, sir.

Crumley hesitates. To his horror, he realises that
Corporal Nobbs, against all expectation, has a point.

                    VERNON CRUMLEY
          Could you not do it surreptitiously?

                    CORPORAL NOBBS
          Ah, well, surreption, yes, we could
          give that a try . . .

The sentence hangs in the air with its hand out.

                    VERNON CRUMLEY
               (finally getting it)
          You won't find me ungrateful.

INT. CRUMLEY'S DEPARTMENT STORE/FIRST FLOOR - NIGHT

Nobbs and Visit emerge from the stairs and walk into
the first floor, which is a mob.

                    CONSTABLE VISIT
          In Omnia we call Hogswatchnight the
          Fast of St Ossory.

They stand aside hurriedly as two children scuttle down
the stairs carrying a large toy boat between them.
Constable Visit visibly grimaces with disgust.

                    CONSTABLE VISIT
          But it is not an occasion for
          superstition and crass commercialism.

Corporal Nobbs eyes the children gloomily.

                    CORPORAL NOBBS
          I used to hang up my stocking every
          Hogswatch, regular. All that ever
          happened was my dad was sick in it
          once.

He removes his helmet. There is the sudden gleam in his
eye.

                    CORPORAL NOBBS
          I'm going in.

INT. TOOTH FAIRY'S CASTLE/FOOT OF TOWER – DAY

Sideney buries his head back in his spell book, muttering an incantation virtually to himself.

Suddenly the pages of his book flick over at great speed, as if a strong gust of wind has swept by. Sideney almost drops the book. There is the sound of falling teeth.

From higher in the pile, teeth are starting to jump off the pile and fall out of the chalk circle.

Teatime looks towards the wizard.

> MR SIDENEY
> There seems to be a thaumic surge . . .
> from somewhere . . .

Sideney fluffs as Teatime leans in. The wizard's thumb heads for his mouth.

> MR SIDENEY
> . . . as if something is triggering
> random bursts of stray belief . . .

Teatime leans very close . . . and he isn't smiling.

INT. CRUMLEY'S DEPARTMENT STORE/GROTTO – NIGHT

Now DEATH's on a roll. A SMALL GIRL is hurried away happy, tottering under the weight of a large fluffy orang-utan.

> DEATH
> IT'S THE EXPRESSION ON THEIR LITTLE
> FACES I LIKE.

> ALBERT
> You mean sort of fear and awe and not
> knowing whether to laugh, cry or wet
> their pants?

> DEATH
> YES. NOW THAT IS WHAT I CALL BELIEF.

DEATH turns back to the Children.

> DEATH
> NEXT! AND WHAT'S YOUR NAME, LITTLE . . .

He hesitates, but rallies, and continues . . .

```
                    DEATH
       . . . PERSON?

                 NOBBY NOBBS
        Nobby Nobbs, Hogfather.
```

Corporal Nobb's face crinkles as he sits on a knee much
bonier than it should be.

```
                    DEATH
        AND HAVE YOU BEEN A GOOD BO . . . A
        GOOD DWA . . . A GOOD GNO . . . A GOOD
        INDIVIDUAL?
```

Nobb's POV . . . is somehow unable to look away from
the intimidating view of the HOGFATHER's face.

And suddenly Nobby finds he has no control at all of
his tongue.

```
                 CORPORAL NOBBS
           's.
```

Nobby's face is fixed
in a grin.

INT. TOOTH FAIRY'S CASTLE/FOOT OF TOWER - NIGHT

Hundreds of teeth
are now jumping from
the pile and out of
the circle. The gang
are frantically
brushing the teeth
back in.

Teatime backs
Sideney, who has his
thumb in his mouth,
towards the pile.

```
        TEATIME
          (smiling)
        So why
        isn't it
        working?
```

Sideney leans back,
nervously and then looks down.

                    MR SIDENEY
          . . . the chalk just got a bit scuffed
          when we were piling up the . . .

He can't bring himself to say it.

                    MR SIDENEY
          . . . the things.

                    TEATIME
          You're sure that's what it is?

                    MR SIDENEY
          Well . . .

                    TEATIME
          What about the spell?

                    MR SIDENEY
          Oh, it'll keep going for ever. The
          simple ones do. It's just a state
          change, powered by the . . . the . . .
          it just keeps going . . .

He swallows and raises a shaking arm again.

                    TEATIME
          Well that's very good, Mr Sideney,
          because if this sympathetic magic
          doesn't work, you will find me very . . .
          unsympathetic.

Sideney sucks on his thumb, hard.

INT. CRUMLEY'S DEPARTMENT STORE/STAIRS - NIGHT

Corporal Nobbs barges his way through the crowds
carrying a very large and unusually shaped present.

He only stops when he is fielded by Constable Visit.

                    CONSTABLE VISIT
          What happened? What happened?

Nobbs shows Constable Visit the present. Visit looks
horrified.

                    CONSTABLE VISIT
          This is disgusting, this whole
          business. It's the worship of idols . . .

Nobbs claws at the raven-bedecked paper to reveal . . .

CORPORAL NOBBS
It's a genuine Burleigh and
Stronginthearm double-action triple-
cantilever crossbow with a polished
walnut stock and engraved silver
facings!

It finally dawns on Constable Visit that something
behind him is amiss.

CONSTABLE VISIT
Aren't we going to arrest this
impostor, corporal?

Corporal Nobbs looks blearily at him through the mists
of possessive pride.

CORPORAL NOBBS
You're foreign, Washpot. I can't expect
you to know the real meaning of
Hogswatch.

INT. DEATH'S HOUSE/LIBRARY - NIGHT

Blood and hooves flicker in front of
Susan's face from the scroll.

SUSAN
So, for the sun to come up
tomorrow morning the
Hogfather must be alive.

RAVEN (O.C.)
Precisemento.

SUSAN
But what if he's dead?

Susan reaches out for the last book
and tries to open it at random . . .
She looks down as there is a rush of
noise and distorted images: hooves,
blood, snow, Massive Bones of Ice and
night . . .

Susan is suddenly THROWN BACK against
the wall. The book drops and slams
shut.

The Raven's feathers are ruffled.

Susan is slumped against the book
case.

INT. UNSEEN UNIVERSITY/HEX'S ROOM

HEX, a large engine, or THINKING MACHINE, dominates the room. It has been draped in holly and someone has put a paper hat on the big glass dome containing the main ant heap.

The Burar is sitting in front of the thing. Sat next to him by a large wooden keyboard is Ponder Stibbons, the Unseen University's TOKEN SANE PERSON.

Ridcully knocks the ashes out of his pipe on Hex's 'Anthill Inside' sticker, causing Ponder to wince.

> RIDCULLY
> This thing's a kind of big
> artificial brain, then?

> PONDER STIBBONS
> You could think of it like
> that. Of course, Hex doesn't
> actually think. Not as such.
> It just appears to be
> thinking.

> RIDCULLY
> Amazin'. So . . . he just
> gives the impression of
> thinking but really it's
> just a show?

> PONDER STIBBONS
> Er . . . yes.

> RIDCULLY
> Just like everyone else,
> then, really.

Ridcully puts his pipe back in his pocket . . . and in the process feels something else there. It's the Verruca Gnome. Ridcully pulls him out.

> RIDCULLY
> I knew I'd come here for something.
> This here chappie is the Verruca Gnome
> . . .

> VERRUCA GNOME
> (shyly)
> Hello.

RIDCULLY
. . . who seems to have popped into
existence to be with us here on
Hogswatchnight. What with the Hogfather
whizzin' around and all the old year's
occult rubbish pilin' up. Just thought
you fellows might check up on this.

PONDER STIBBONS
A Verruca Gnome?

The gnome clutches his sack protectively.

RIDCULLY
Makes about as much sense as a lot of
things, I suppose. After all, there's
a Tooth Fairy, ain' there? You
might as well wonder why we have a
God of Wine and not a God of
Hangovers . . .

He stops. There is a
glingleglingleglingle sound.

RIDCULLY
Anyone else hear that
noise just then?

PONDER STIBBONS
Sorry, Archchancellor?

RIDCULLY
Sort of
glingleglingleglingle? Like
little tinkly bells?

PONDER STIBBONS
Didn't hear anything like
that, sir.

RIDCULLY
Oh.

Ridcully shrugs.

RIDCULLY
Anyway . . . what was I
saying . . . yes . . . no
one's ever heard of a Verruca
Gnome until tonight.

                        VERRUCA GNOME
            That's right. Even I've never heard of
            me until tonight, and I'm me.

                        PONDER STIBBONS
            We'll see what Hex can find out,
            Archchancellor.

                            RIDCULLY
            Good man.

Ridcully puts the gnome back in his pocket and looks up
at Hex.

Ponder taps at the huge wooden keyboard and then nods
to one of the students, who pulls a large red LEVER
marked 'Do Not Pull'.

Gears spin, somewhere inside Hex. Little trap-doors
open in the ant farms and millions of ants began to
scurry along the networks of glass tubing . . .

INT. DEATH'S HOUSE/LIBRARY – NIGHT

Susan is lying prostrate. The Raven is standing on her
forehead with his beak poised above one of her
eyeballs. He shrugs his shoulders.

                            RAVEN
            At least she won't be needing these any
                                    more . . .

Just as he raises his head . . .

Susan's eyes slam open. The Raven jumps in the air.

                    RAVEN
          Can't blame a bird for trying!

Susan rubs her head then looks down gravely at the
book.

                    SUSAN
          He was at the Castle of Bones.

She gets up, goes over to the desk and picks up DEATH's
sword. Its thin blue blade flashes through the air.

EXT. SKY - NIGHT

The sleigh soars into the snowy sky. Albert finally
gets the roll-up in his mouth and tries to light it.

                    DEATH
          ON THE WHOLE, I THINK THAT WENT VERY
          WELL, DON'T YOU?

                    ALBERT
          Yes, master.

                    DEATH
          AND I THINK I'VE GOT THE LAUGH WORKING
          REALLY WELL NOW. HO. HO. HO.

                    ALBERT
          Yeah, sir, very jolly. Tomorrow morning
          they're going to believe, all right.

                    DEATH
            (suddenly grave)
          IF THEY DON'T BELIEVE . . . THEN THERE
          WON'T BE A TOMORROW MORNING . . .

And with that DEATH snaps the reins . . . just as
Albert's roll-up is finally alight. Before he can take
a puff it's blown clean out of his mouth.

The HOGS surge and pull the sleigh off into the sky.

. . . as the Auditors materialise and watch them go.

                    AUDITOR 2
          His plan might work, you know.

                    AUDITOR 3
          Only if Teatime fails.

                    AUDITOR 4
          But what about the granddaughter?

                    AUDITOR 1
          Once the spell is cast, her success
          probability will be, as near as is
          practicably calculable, nil.

EXT. THE CASTLE OF BONES - NIGHT

The Castle of Bones looms above us. Its dramatic
pillars of ice lead into a huge covered entrance beyond
which it narrows to a smaller hallway. In the distance,
at the far end of the hallway, an ice-sculpted throne
of bones can just be seen. The whole structure appears
to be groaning and creaking.

INT. THE CASTLE OF BONES/ENTRANCE - NIGHT

The castle looks like a giant mausoleum.

A huge piece of ice falls from the roof. It crashes
into the snow behind the columns, lifting a massive
plume of snow dust into the air.

As it drifts away in the wind we see Susan dismounting
from Binky and walking into the creaking danger.

A little way beyond the pillars she finds the very
large slab of ice, cracked into pieces. Far above,
stars are visible through the hole it has left in the
roof. As she looks up, a few small lumps of ice thump
into a snowdrift.

Snow has blown over the ice. Susan looks down at the
drifts. There are the faint outlines of booted
footprints. And . . . half obscured by the snow . . .
it looks as though a sleigh has stood here. Animals
have milled around. But the snow is covering
everything.

Susan bends down and finds footprints in the snow.
Albert's roll-up tobacco is everywhere.

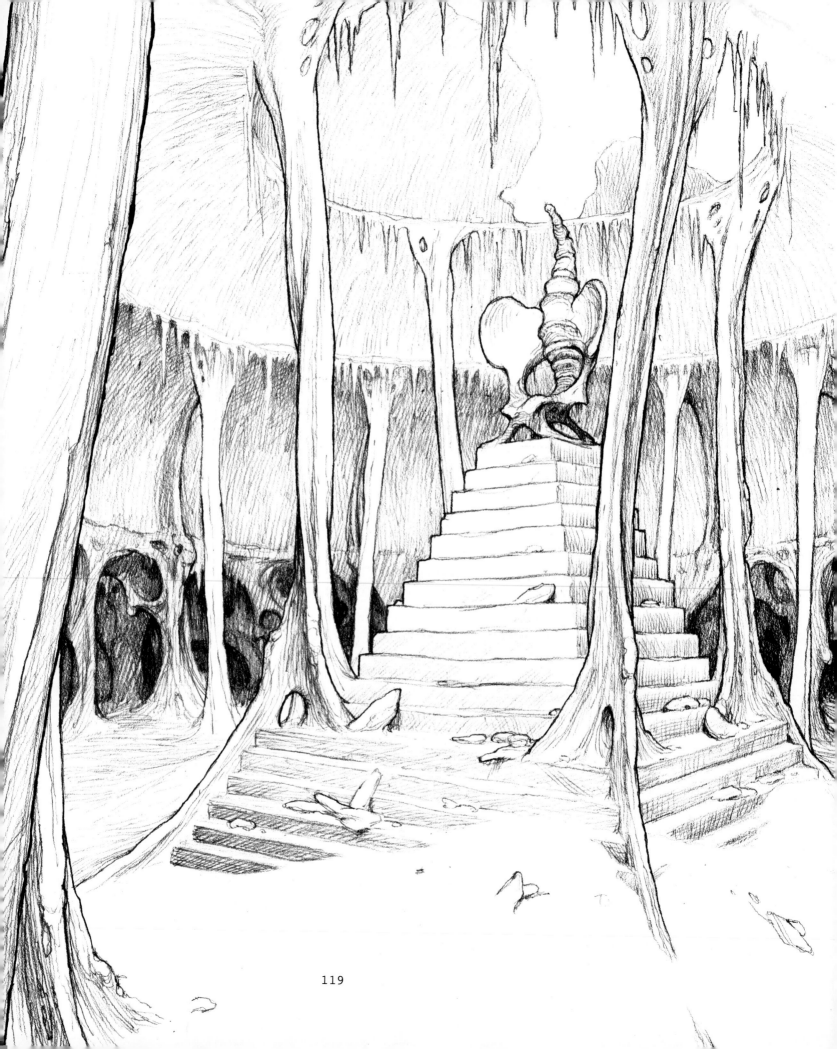

> SUSAN
> (to herself)
> I don't see the Hogfather as someone
> who rolls his own.

She stands and heads off into the gloom.

Susan follows them into the narrowing hallway.

INT. GAITER'S HOUSE/SCHOOL ROOM - NIGHT

A pair of HOGFATHER BOOTS bearing tusks that curl up
from the sole at the front land with a thump on a rug.
A sack of presents clumps down next to them.

INT. GAITER'S HOUSE/TWYLA'S BEDROOM - NIGHT

We hear a distant thump. A small hand and then Twyla's
face emerges from under the blankets. She hears another
bumping sound from downstairs.

Gawain stirs. They both look towards their door and
listen.

INT. TOOTH FAIRY'S CASTLE/FOOT OF TOWER - DAY

Sideney waves his wand with
a final flourish of his
arms towards the pile of
teeth.

There is a pause as the
gang look on. Nothing seems
to be happening.

> TEATIME
> And this was going
> to be your big
> moment.

Sideney's thumb heads for
his mouth. Teatime's blade
is there in a flash.

> TEATIME
> Such a shame.

The gang look away from
Sideney, preparing to wince.

                    BANJO (O.C.)
         Pretty lights.

Banjo is still looking at the teeth, his mouth gaping
open.

Starting at the bottom of the pile, the teeth are
starting to GLOW . . . magically.

Sideney's thumb drops from his mouth, which begins to
smile.

Teatime turns towards the teeth.

                         TEATIME
          Think happy, Banjo.

Banjo smiles on command . . . and so does Teatime.

INT. GAITER'S HOUSE/SCHOOL ROOM - NIGHT

A red-gloved hand picks up a pork pie, but as it does
it knocks over a glass of sherry. The glass falls in
SLOW MOTION, spilling the amber liquid over a letter to
the Hogfather . . .

INT. GAITER'S HOUSE/PASSAGE - NIGHT

Twyla and Gawain in their pyjamas creep towards the
nursery. They hear a smash of glass and stop.

                         TWYLA
               (excited)
          It's him!

INT. THE CASTLE OF BONES/THRONE ROOM - NIGHT

Ahead of Susan a pyramid of steps, with a big chair on
top, rises majestically above her. Snow falls through a
chasm-like hole high above it.

In the snow beneath it there are a lot of Albert-shaped
footprints.

Behind her, a pillar groans and twists slightly.

Susan bends down and pulls at something half-buried in
the snow. It is a red-and-white-striped candy cane.

She kicks the snow aside elsewhere and finds a wooden toy soldier.

She probes further and finds a broken trumpet.

There is some more groaning in the darkness.

Susan looks further into the darkness but can see nothing.

The column nearest her creaks loudly, twists, and a fine haze of ice crystals drops from the roof . . . followed by a large shard of ice that crashes into the snow right beside her.

She turns to leave and hears the groan again. She stops. It isn't dissimilar to the tortured sounds being made by the ice, except that ice, after all, doesn't moan.

>   VOICE IN SNOW (O.C.)
>   Oh, me . . .

Susan hesitates and takes one step towards the sound.

Another shard of ice slams into the snow where she was just stood. Melt-water is now flowing from above.

Susan bites her lip and looks in the direction of the voice. Then she looks back to the way out . . . as the whole building seems to shudder and quake . . .

INT. TOOTH FAIRY'S CASTLE/FOOT OF TOWER - DAY

The whole of the massive pile of teeth glows a magical glow which surges even more strongly . . .

. . . sending a wave of warm light across the faces of the watching gang.

>   TEATIME
>   If I can just find her . . .

Teatime stops looking at Banjo and turns to Mr Brown.

>   TEATIME
>   . . . There's one door you haven't
>   found. Find it.

Mr Brown takes his bag and grumpily stumps off.

                    TEATIME
         . . . then just think what I can make
         the kiddiwinkies think.

INT. SUSAN'S HOUSE/SCHOOL ROOM - NIGHT

Twyla and Gawain peek their heads around the door.

The figure in the red fur coat is on his knees mopping
up sherry. A small plume of smoke floats from the red
hood.

Twyla harrumphs.

                    TWYLA
              You're not the
              Hogfather.

The figure looks over his
shoulder. The hood slips back
from his head to reveal MR
GAITER, complete with cigar.

                    GAWAIN
              (horrified)
              Daddy!

On the mantelpiece the CLOCK is
just before 12. Hanging beneath
it, in Twyla's pink stocking, the
DOLLY has GONE . . .

INT. THE CASTLE OF BONES/THRONE ROOM - NIGHT

Susan runs . . .

. . . TOWARDS the groaning, moaning figure lying
spread-eagled in a snowdrift. She almost misses it
because it is only just visible in the snow.

                    SUSAN
              Are you all right?

The recumbent figure opens its eyes and stares straight
up.

                    YOUNG MAN
              (moaning)
              I wish I was dead . . .

A piece of ice the size of a house falls down in the far depths of the building and explodes in a shower of sharp little shards.

> SUSAN
> You may have come to the right place.

The young man watches more falling ice and looks very, very pale.

EXT. SKY ABOVE ANKH-MORPORK - NIGHT

DEATH urges the hogs on. Something small drops into his hand.

There is a moment of horrible silence as they both stare at the lifetimer.

DEATH looks at Albert, who looks worried.

> DEATH
> DUTY CALLS.

> ALBERT
> Yes, but which one?

DEATH pulls on the reins and turns the sleigh around . . .

INT. TOOTH FAIRY'S CASTLE/FOOT OF TOWER - DAY

The glowing pile of teeth is reflected in Teatime's glass eye. As he looks up, the CAMERA cranes up, revealing his smiling face.

> TEATIME
> Happy Hogwash, everybody.

From high above the pile, the light from the teeth spills and bounces chaotically around the white walls.

INT. THE CASTLE OF BONES/THRONE ROOM - NIGHT

Susan grabs the young man under his arms and hauls him out of the snow.

She does her best to prop him up as, swaying and
slipping, they make their way back to the exit. Above
them a massive fissure opens up in the roof with a
rending, cracking sound.

                    YOUNG MAN
          My head . . .

Susan looks up and quickly back down to the young man.

                    SUSAN
               (confused)
          Are you . . . ?

Susan looks more closely at the boy.

                    SUSAN
          . . . the Hogf—?

The ice above them creaks with a sound like thunder,
drowning Susan out. Then silence.

                    YOUNG MAN
          I feel awful. Have you
          got any ice?

With which . . . the Castle of
Bones falls in.

EXT. THE CASTLE OF BONES - NIGHT

The collapse of the building is
stately and impressive, and
seems to go on for a long time.
Pillars fall in, the slabs of
the roof slide down, the ice
crackles and splinters. The air
above the tumbling wreckage
fills with a haze of snow and
ice crystals. The sound is
almost deafening.

But the fate of our heroine,
her mysterious new friend, the
rat and the raven . . . is
unknown . . .

END OF PART 1

Terry Pratchett's

HOGFATHER

The Illustrated Screenplay

PART TWO

WRITTEN FOR THE SCREEN

BY VADIM JEAN

MUCKED AROUND WITH

BY TERRY PRATCHETT

FINAL SHOOTING SCRIPT

INT. TOOTH FAIRY'S CASTLE/FOOT OF TOWER - DAY

The PILE OF TEETH glows, emanating magic.

INT. GAITER'S HOUSE/SCHOOL ROOM - NIGHT

The mantel clock strikes MIDNIGHT.

Mr Gaiter's mouth drops open. The cigar falls from his
teeth as he scrabbles to pull his Hogfather costume
hood back up.

Twyla and Gawain are dumbstruck.

> MR GAITER
> I say, it's not what you think.

> TWYLA
> Yes it is.

Mr Gaiter bows his head.

On the mantelpiece we can see that in the images on the
HOGSWATCH CARDS the Hogfather's face is
beginning to TURN INTO MR GAITER's. At the
window . . .

EXT. GAITER'S HOUSE - NIGHT

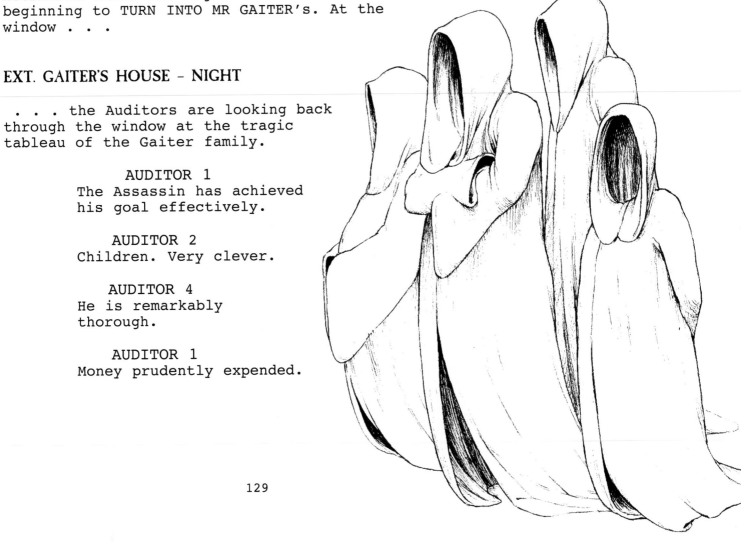

. . . the Auditors are looking back
through the window at the tragic
tableau of the Gaiter family.

> AUDITOR 1
> The Assassin has achieved
> his goal effectively.

> AUDITOR 2
> Children. Very clever.

> AUDITOR 4
> He is remarkably
> thorough.

> AUDITOR 1
> Money prudently expended.

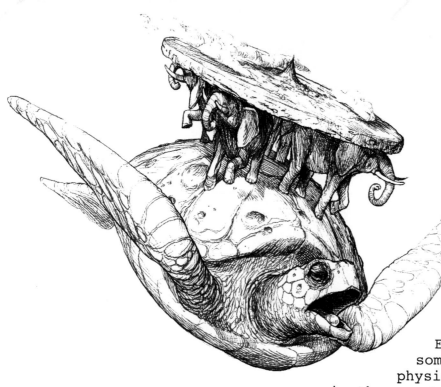

AUDITOR 2
Dare I conjecture
what he might turn
his talents to
next?

With which they
evaporate into the snowy
night.

EXT. SPACE - NIGHT

Mists roll, stars peek,
glinting faintly through.

NARRATOR (V.O.)
Everything starts
somewhere, although many
physicists disagree. There
is the constant desire to find out
where, where is the point where it all
began . . .

Gaps begin to appear in the mists and in the distance
we can just make out an odd shape.

NARRATOR (V.O.)
But much, much later than that . . .
the Discworld was formed . . .

Slowly the mists part and we begin to see . . .

NARRATOR (V.O.)
. . . drifting onwards through space
atop four elephants on the shell of a
giant turtle, The Great A'Tuin.

We begin to fly towards the Turtle.

NARRATOR (V.O.)
And it was some time after its creation
when most people forgot that the very
oldest stories of the beginning are,
sooner or later, about blood . . . at
least, that's one theory . . .

And now we're flying through the clouds above the disc
itself.

NARRATOR (V.O.)
. . . The philosopher Didactylos has

suggested an alternative hypothesis:
'Things just happen. What the hell'.

And onwards over the city and down towards the centre . . .

> NARRATOR (V.O.)
> Our story began in Ankh-Morpork, the
> twin city of proud Ankh and pestilent
> Morpork, the biggest city in Discworld
> . . .

. . . And we continue to a street where, with a
sprinkle of magic and a 'twing', we appear to travel
through a narrow sparkly gate in a wall . . .

> NARRATOR (V.O.)
> . . . but now takes us to the
> Tooth Fairy's castle . . .

INT. TOOTH FAIRY'S CASTLE/FOOT OF TOWER – DAY

The tower is a hollow tube. Four spiral
staircases climb the inside, criss-crossing
on landings and occasionally passing
through one another in defiance of
generally accepted physics.

> NARRATOR (V.O.)
> . . . where our story continues to
> be much sooner, rather than
> later,

But . . . there is an absence of
shadows. The white marble-like stone
seems to glow from the inside. It is as
if the tower seems to avoid darkness.

> NARRATOR (V.O.)
> . . . about blood.

INT. TOOTH FAIRY'S CASTLE/MONEY ROOM – NIGHT

Medium Dave Lilywhite hauls another
bag of money towards the door.

> MEDIUM DAVE
> There must be thousands here . . .

                    CHICKENWIRE
          And what's all this stuff?

Chickenwire opens a box.

                    CHICKENWIRE
          's just paper.

He tosses it aside.

                    MEDIUM DAVE
              (smirking)
          They're title deeds for properties. And
          they're better than money.

                    CHICKENWIRE
          If we steal them, do they become ours?

                    MEDIUM DAVE
          Is that a trick question?

                    CHICKENWIRE
          Anyway, let's get going. He won't
          miss a . . .

                    VOICE (O.C.)
          Gentlemen . . .

They turn. Teatime is in the doorway.

                    CHICKENWIRE
          We were just . . . we were just
          piling up the stuff.

Teatime laughs. Chickenwire laughs. Even
Medium Dave laughs.

And then Teatime is on Dave, pushing him
irresistibly backwards until he hits the
wall, his feet lifted off the ground
like a feather.

There is a blur. Dave tries to blink but suddenly his
left eyelid is bleeding.

Teatime's 'good' eye is close to him. The pupil is a
dot.

The knife is right by Medium Dave's face, the point of
the blade the merest fraction of an inch from his right
eye.

TEATIME
          (whispering)
     I know people say I'd kill them as soon
     as look at them. And in fact I'd much
     rather kill you than look at you, Mr
     Lilywhite.

He relaxes a little, but his hand still holds the knife
to Medium Dave's unblinking eye.

          TEATIME
     You're thinking that Banjo is
     going to help you. That's how
     it's always been, isn't it? But
     Banjo is my friend now.

Medium Dave's POV. He manages to focus
beyond Teatime's ear. His brother is
just standing there, with a blank face.

          TEATIME
     Banjo has the heart of a little
     child.

The others are frozen in place.

          TEATIME
     I believe I have, too.

The knife disappears somewhere about
his clothing.

Medium Dave slumps down.

          TEATIME
     Help him, Banjo.

On cue, Banjo lumbers forward and
helps his brother up.

          TEATIME
     As far as this goes . . .

He kicks a sack. It splits open. Silver and copper fall
in an expensive trickle.

          TEATIME
     . . . I really have no use for it.
     It's only pillow money.

The gang watch the coins roll across the floor.

                    TEATIME
Something much more
interesting has become
apparent. Hasn't it, Banjo?
Drop him.

Banjo lets his brother fall to the
ground.

                    TEATIME
Control. Control the inner
child and it'll even give
you its teeth.

The gang look at Banjo, with his
gap-toothed smile.

                    TEATIME
And somewhere in this tower
you're going to help me
find someone who can use it
to give me the world.

He stands back and smiles happily.

From high up in the tower a voice
shouts out.

Teatime goes out onto the stairs.
Still visible from the room he
moves to the edge of the
staircase, leans out and looks
up.

                    CHICKENWIRE
        (whispering)
Was he saying we could take the money
and go?

                    MEDIUM DAVE
Don't be bloody stupid.

INT. TOOTH FAIRY'S CASTLE/STAIRS - DAY

Teatime cranes to look up the tower.

                    MR BROWN (O.C.)
Mr Teh-ah-time-eh!

Mr Brown's head appears from higher up.

Teatime looks back into the room and nods to the gang
to follow him. He starts up the stairs.

Medium Dave still clutches his face as the gang follow.

EXT. THE CASTLE OF BONES - NIGHT

The fog of ice settles and there is nothing but drifted
snow.

In the foreground, the crimson of spilt blood soaks
into the pure white of strange foot-prints, half human,
half animal in the snow. We PULL FOCUS to the
background where . . . the Castle of Bones used to be.
It is eerily silent, as if the Hogfather's house was
never there.

The CAMERA pans around to the edge of the forest.

A layer of snow from a fir tree
falls to the snowy ground. Then
silence once more until . . .

Suddenly an eye ball appears in the
snow. Then a crown of vine leaves
lifts out of the snow on the head
of the boy — BILIOUS. He clears the
snow from his eyes.

Then SUSAN also struggles out from
under the snow.

> BILIOUS
> That was amazing.

Susan takes in the site of their
near-disaster.

> SUSAN
> As though it never
> existed.

She turns to the groaning figure.

> SUSAN
> What were you doing there?

> BILIOUS
> I don't know. I just
> opened my eyes and there
> I was.

SUSAN

Who are you?

BILIOUS

I . . . think my name is Bilious. I'm
the . . . I'm the oh God of Hangovers.

SUSAN

There's a God of Hangovers?

BILIOUS

An oh God. When people witness me, you
see, they clutch their head and say,
'Oh God . . .'

SUSAN

I've never heard of a God of Hangovers
. . .

BILIOUS
You've heard of Bibulous,
the God of Wine? Big fat
man, wears vine leaves
round his head. Well, you
know why he's so cheerful?
It's because it's me that
. . .

SUSAN
. . . gets the
hangovers?

BILIOUS
I don't even drink!

Bilious sways back and forth.

SUSAN
What were you doing in
there?

BILIOUS
I don't know. Where was there exactly?

Susan looks back at where the castle was. It has
entirely gone.

SUSAN
That was the Hogfather's house.

The oh God nods carefully.

                    BILIOUS
          I often see things that weren't there a
          moment ago and they often aren't there
          a moment later . . .

                    SUSAN
          We've got to find out what's happened
          to him.

                    BILIOUS
          Excuse me, I think I'm about to throw
          up . . .

Bilious starts to look faint.

                    SUSAN
          You must be able to remember what
          happened here. And I need you to help
          me . . .

He heads for the trees, but folds up and lands in the
snow again.

                    SUSAN
          You're a long streak of widdle, aren't
          you?

Susan shakes her head, picks the oh God up, puts him
over her shoulder and moves off.

The wind rattles in the trees behind them. Snow slides
off branches. Somewhere in the dark there is a flurry
of hooves. From the edge of the frozen forest . . .
animal eyes watch them go . . . animal eyes and a flash
of what could just be a SNOUT and a pair of TUSKS . . .

INT. TOOTH FAIRY'S CASTLE/LOWER STAIRS - DAY

The gang reach a complicated landing. Sideney takes an
intake of breath as he finds he has to walk up the next
flight by stepping down the underside of a stair so
that the distant floor now hangs overhead like a
ceiling.

The gang shut their eyes when they take this step.

Teatime takes these stairs three at a time, laughing
like a kid with a new toy.

                       137

INT. TOOTH FAIRY'S CASTLE/ANTE-ROOM BALCONY - DAY

Teatime, Sideney and the gang find Mr Brown by a locked door. The locksmith's pick turns the last tumbler. Mr Brown looks through an elaborate-looking device into the lock.

>   MR BROWN
>   He's barricaded himself in.

Teatime stands back.

>   TEATIME
>   Banjo, a little job for a good boy.

INT. TOOTH FAIRY'S CASTLE/TOOTH FAIRY'S ANTE-ROOM - DAY

The guard is cowering behind a pillar. He cringes back as Teatime moves towards him.

>   GUARD
>   I'm not telling you anything. Who are
>   you anyway?

>   TEATIME
>   (cheerfully)
>   Ah, I'm glad you asked. I'm your worst
>   nightmare!

The guard shudders.

>   GUARD
>   You mean . . .
>   the one with
>   the giant
>   cabbage and the
>   sort of
>   whirring knife
>   thing?

>   TEATIME
>   (nonplussed)
>   Sorry? No, not
>   that one.

Teatime withdraws a dagger from his sleeve.

                        TEATIME
              I'm the one where this man comes out of
              nowhere and kills you stone dead.

The guard grins with relief.

                        GUARD
               Oh, that one. But that one's not very
               . . .

He crumples around Teatime's suddenly outthrust fist.
And then, just like the other guards, he fades.

                        TEATIME
               Rather a charitable act there, I feel.

Teatime watches as the man vanishes.

                        TEATIME
               But it is nearly Hogswatch, after all.

Teatime turns to see . . .

    . . . an ordinary-looking LARGE DOOR in the wall
behind the fallen cabinet. It is covered with many
ELABORATE LOCKS.

Teatime smiles.

                        TEATIME
               Bring me the girl.

EXT. ROOF TOP OF UNSEEN UNIVERSITY - NIGHT

The runners of the Hogfather's sleigh hit the roof.
DEATH pulls out a Lifetimer from his cloak.

                        DEATH
               ODD.

He looks down.

Someone, a corpse, is lying in the snow. A TOOTH-SHAPED
HELMET is just about on his head. On his shirt is a
badge with what looks like a DRAWING OF A TOOTH on it.

Albert looks down at the snow-covered corpse.

ALBERT
It's a scythe job, then?

DEATH swings his scythe.

The spirit of the man looks down at himself. Then he
stares from himself to Albert to DEATH and his phantom
expression goes from shock to concern.

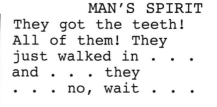

                                    MAN'S SPIRIT
                            They got the teeth!
                            All of them! They
                            just walked in . . .
                            and . . . they
                            . . . no, wait . . .

                            He fades and is gone.

                            Albert squints up at the sky.
                            Then he looks around,
                            puzzled.

                                    ALBERT
                            Where did he come
                            from?

                                    DEATH
                            A PLACE I CANNOT GO.

                            Albert looks a little
                            confused.

                                    DEATH
                            THERE'S NO PLACE FOR
                            ME IN A CHILD'S WORLD.

                                    ALBERT
                            Well, even if you
                            could go there, we've
                            got our work cut out
                            just keeping the
                            Hogfather's seat warm
                            here.

                                    DEATH
                            IF WHAT'S HAPPENING IN
                            THE TOOTH FAIRY'S
                            CASTLE ISN'T STOPPED
                            THEN ALL THIS WILL BE A
                            WASTE OF TIME.
DEATH looks more closely at the guard's
tooth badge.

                    DEATH
          AND IF THEY GET TO THE TOOTH FAIRY,
          THEY WILL BE ABLE TO CONTROL ALL HUMAN
          BELIEF.

DEATH gathers up the reins.

                    DEATH
          UNLESS SUSAN GETS THERE FIRST.

DEATH snaps the reins and the hogs pull the sleigh into
the night sky.

INT. UNSEEN UNIVERSITY/GREAT HALL - NIGHT

Ridcully stands in the middle of the floor surveying
the hall.

There is a hammering on the outer door.

The Archchancellor opens it.

Then a hooded figure steps in, carrying a limp bundle
over its shoulder.

Ridcully notices that the
robe has lace around the
bottom, and the hood is
rather stylish, in the
mode of the classic
Victorian governess.

Then the hood is pushed
back. It's Susan.

               SUSAN
          I need your help,
          Mr Ridcully.

               RIDCULLY
          You're . . .
          aren't you . . . ?

               SUSAN
          Yes, the scythe,
          the cloak, the
          white horse, the
          talents . . . the
          granddaughter.

                    RIDCULLY
        And . . . are you here on business?

Ridcully waggles his eyebrows towards the slumbering
figure over her shoulder.

                    SUSAN
        I need you to wake him up.

Ridcully lifts the oh God's head. There's a groan.

                    SUSAN
        He's the oh God of Hangovers.

The wizards grimace at the thought.

                    SUSAN
        Something nasty's happening tonight.
        I'm hoping he can tell me what it is.
        But he's got to be able to think
        straight first.

                    RIDCULLY
        And you brought him here?

Susan's beginning to wonder.

EXT. UNSEEN UNIVERSITY/ROOF - NIGHT

A garret window in the roof opens. The sound of student
revelry spills out, followed by the head of a
dishevelled STUDENT WIZARD who pukes into the gleaming
snow. After a bit more retching he looks across the
roof and notices the corpse of the Guard.

The student wizard's face is a mixture of curiosity and
mischief.

INT. TOOTH FAIRY'S CASTLE/TOOTH FAIRY'S ANTE-ROOM - DAY

Teatime has his knife to Violet's throat and forces her
to look at the mysterious entrance, which is making her
so nervous she won't stop talking, so their dialogue
overlaps.

                    VIOLET
        Why are you doing this? I was a bit
        behind with the teeth I know . . .

                    TEATIME
          Is she behind this door?

                    VIOLET
          I don't know . . . and there was
          nearly thirteen dollars in pillow money
          owing, I admit, but . . .

                    TEATIME
          Is this her door?

                    VIOLET
          . . . I signed the form GV19 for Bulk
          Collection and Despatch . . .

Teatime pushes the knife a little harder into her throat.

                    TEATIME
          Will you just shut up and answer the
          question?

Violet finally stops for a moment.

                    VIOLET
          I don't know. I've never been here
          before.

                    TEATIME
          Then your boss probably doesn't realise
          how irritating you are.

Teatime pushes Violet towards the door, knife still at
her throat.

                    TEATIME
          Come out, come out, wherever you are . . .

Another little nudge of the blade and Violet shrieks
again.

                    TEATIME
          . . . or Miss Bottler gets it.

                    VIOLET
          It was only a bit of loose change and
          . . .

Teatime closes his eyes as Violet's terrified chatter
carries on and on . . .

EXT. SNOWFIELD - NIGHT

Albert and DEATH fly over snowy fields. Albert is
trying to light a roll-up cigarette. He just gets it
lit when . . .

The reins are hauled so sharply and so quickly that
Albert's roll-up flies out of his mouth before he can
take a puff and the hogs end up facing the other way.

Albert fights his way out of a drift of teddy bears.

> ALBERT
> Will you stop doing that!

DEATH points downwards. An endless white snowfield lies
below, with the occasional glow from a candlelit
window.

Albert is only just hanging on as the sleigh tumbles
downwards.

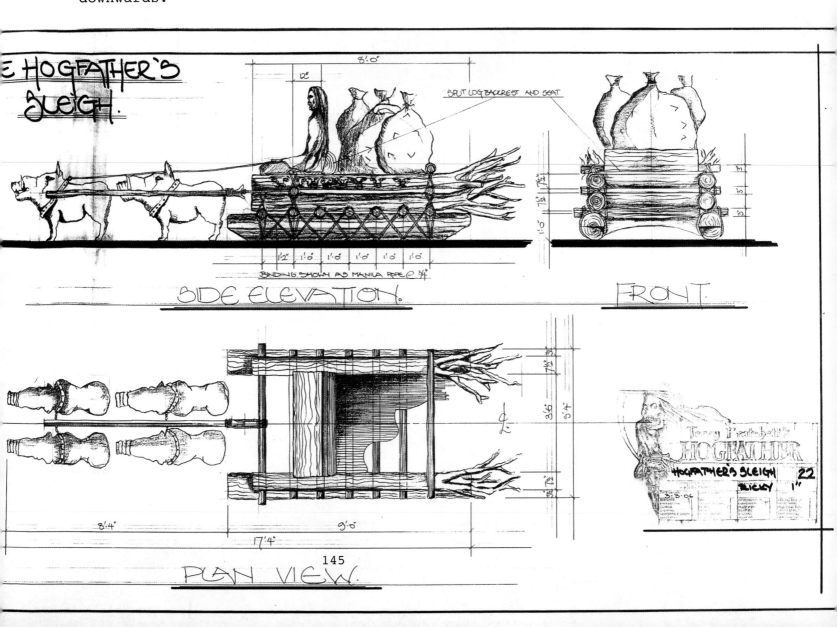

EXT. SCROTE SHACK – NIGHT

The shack is pretty isolated. It is a small dot in the middle of the Plains.

EXT. SCROTE SHACK – NIGHT

Albert is stood by the chimney, shouting down inside.

> ALBERT
> Sam Scrote, aged eight.

There are the clattering sounds of bone on brick from   within.

Albert's feet slip a little in the snow . . .

INT. SCROTE SHACK – NIGHT

The house has an iron stove. Voices echo faintly within the pipe.

> DEATH (O.C.)
> THIS IS REALLY, REALLY STUPID.

The second voice sounds as though it comes from someone standing on the roof and shouting down the pipe.

> ALBERT (O.C)
> I think the tradition got started when everyone had them big chimneys, master.

> DEATH (O.C.)
> INDEED? IT'S ONLY A MERCY IT'S
> UNLIT.

There is some muffled scratching and banging, and then a thump from within the pot-belly of the stove. The stove lid is lifted up and pushed sideways. A skeletal arm with a red sleeve comes out and feels around the front of the stove until it finds the handle. It plays with it for a while and then stops.

> ALBERT (O.C)
> It's brass monkeys out here.

The voice sounds pitiful as it echoes down from the
roof. Then there is the sound of bumping, crashing and
a thump from outside the door.

                    ALBERT (O.C)
          Oh bugger.

Albert's voice now sounds a lot closer.

The door opens and Albert enters, dusting the snow from
his legs and peeling the crushed roll-up from his face.

DEATH looks at the sock hooked on to the side of the
stove. It has a hole in it. A letter, in erratic
handwriting, is attached to it. DEATH picks it up.

                    DEATH
          THE BOY WANTS A PAIR OF TROUSERS THAT
          HE DOESN'T HAVE TO SHARE, A HUGE MEAT
          PIE, A SUGAR MOUSE, 'A LOT OF TOYS' AND
          A PUPPY CALLED SCRUFF.

                    ALBERT
          Ah, sweet. I shall wipe away a tear,
          'cos what he's gettin', see, is this
          little wooden toy and an apple.

He holds them out.

                    DEATH
          BUT THE LETTER CLEARLY . . .

                    ALBERT
          Yes, well, it's socio-economic factors
          again, right? The world'd be in a right
          mess if everyone got what they asked
          for, eh?

                    DEATH
          I GAVE THEM WHAT THEY WANTED IN THE
          STORE . . .

                    ALBERT
          What good's a god who gives you
          everything you want?

                    DEATH
          YOU HAVE ME THERE.

                    ALBERT
          It's the hope that's important. Big
          part of belief, hope. Give people jam

today and they'll just sit and eat it.
Jam tomorrow, now - that'll keep them
going for ever.

                    DEATH
AND YOU MEAN THAT BECAUSE OF THIS THE
POOR GET POOR THINGS AND THE RICH GET
RICH THINGS?

                    ALBERT
's right. That's the meaning of
Hogswatch.

DEATH nearly wails.

                    DEATH
BUT I'M THE HOGFATHER!

He looks embarrassed.

                    DEATH
AT THE MOMENT, I MEAN.

Albert starts to roll himself another one of his
horrible thin cigarettes.

                    ALBERT
        (shrugging)
Makes no difference. I remember when I
was a nipper, one Hogswatch I had my
heart set on this huge model horse they
had in the shop . . .

His face creases for a moment in a grim smile of
recollection. And as he does we . . .

                            DISSOLVE TO:

INT. TOYMAKER'S SHOP/PAST - DAY

. . . Albert's face as a small boy. He has his nose up
against the window. It is snowing outside.

The shop door chimes as it opens and a well-dressed
person comes in. Albert's eyes swing over to try to see
them and then back.

EXT. TOYMAKER'S SHOP - DAY

From outside we see past YOUNG ALBERT as . . .

ALBERT (V.O.)
I saw them
take it out of
the window,
someone was in
there buying
it, and,
y'know, just
for a second
I thought it
really was
going to be
for me . . .

INT. TOYMAKER'S SHOP
- DAY

The CAMERA tracks
slowly in on young
Albert's longing
face.

ALBERT (V.O.)
I spent
hours with my nose pressed up against
the window . . . until they heard me
callin', and unfroze me.

And from his face slowly we . . .

DISSOLVE TO:

INT. SCROTE SHACK/PRESENT - NIGHT

Albert's face. He shrugs again.

ALBERT
I'd've killed for that horse. O'
course, I still hung up my stocking on
Hogswatch Eve, and in the morning, you
know what? Our dad had put in this
little horse he'd carved his very own
self . . .

DEATH
AH. AND THAT WAS WORTH MORE THAN ALL
THE EXPENSIVE TOY HORSES IN THE WORLD,
EH?

Albert gives him a beady look.

                              ALBERT
              No. Only grown-ups think like that.
              You're a selfish little bugger when
              you're seven.

Albert leans against the stove and strikes a match.

DEATH looks perturbed.

                              DEATH
              THIS IS WRONG. IT IS . . . UNFAIR.

Albert looks a little out of his depth at this point.

                              ALBERT
              That's life, master.

A draft from down the chimney blows out the match he's
trying to light the cigarette with.

                              DEATH
              BUT I'M NOT.
                (sadly)
              THIS IS SUPPOSED TO BE THE SEASON TO BE
              JOLLY.

He wraps his red robe around him.

                              DEATH
              AND OTHER THINGS ENDING IN OLLY.

Albert shakes his head.

The little ragged stocking is now bulging with a large
MEAT PIE sticking out of the top and . . . it BARKS.

INT. UNSEEN UNIVERSITY/GREAT HALL - NIGHT

The oh God moans. He is laid out on a bench in the
Great Hall. The Senior Wizards gather round, all eager
to help.

                              SUSAN
              If you're the Lecturer in Recent Runes,
              can't you do something more, well,
              magical?

                       LECTURER IN RECENT RUNES
              Spold's Unstirring Divisor would do it.
              You'd end up with a large beaker full
              of all the nastiness. Not difficult at

all, if you don't mind the side-
effects.

                    SUSAN
        (sceptical)
    Tell me about the side-effects.

            LECTURER IN RECENT RUNES
    The main one is that the rest of him
    would end up in a somewhat larger
    beaker.

            SUSAN
        Alive?

The Lecturer in Recent
Runes screws up his
face and waggles his
hands.

    LECTURER IN RECENT
            RUNES
        Broadly, yes.
        Living tissue,
        certainly. And
        definitely sober.

Susan sighs.

            THE DEAN
        Why don't we just
        mix up absolutely
        everything and see
        what happens?

                RIDCULLY
    It's got to be worth a try.

Bilious gulps.

INT. UNSEEN UNIVERSITY/GREAT HALL - LATER

The big glass beaker for the cure is on a pedestal in
the middle of the floor.

The Dean drops in a GREENISH BALL OF LIGHT that sinks
under the surface. The only apparent effect is that it
causes PURPLE BUBBLES to creep over the sides of the
beaker and drip onto the floor.

Bilious looks over at the concoction.

                    BILIOUS
          (firmly)
     I'm not drinking that.

Bilious clutches at his head.

                    RIDCULLY
     It's not quite ready yet.

Bilious groans.

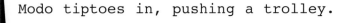

                    Modo tiptoes in, pushing a trolley.

                              RIDCULLY
                    Ah, thank you, Modo.

                    There is a large metal bowl on it,
                    in which a small bottle stands in
                    the middle of a heap of crushed ice.

                              SUSAN
                    Is this going to take much
                    longer? We may not have
                    much time.

                              RIDCULLY
                    You can never be too
                    careful.

                    Ridcully puts down the crystal and
                    fishes a pair of HEAVY GLOVES from
                    his hat . . . and then a WELDING
                    MASK . . .

The wizards are suddenly no longer gathered around
Ridcully, but instead are standing close to various
items of heavy furniture.

Ridcully carefully lifts up the bottle.

                    SUSAN
          What's that?

                    RIDCULLY
     Wow-Wow Sauce. The hottest sauce in the
     universe.

                    THE DEAN
     And it'll blow your head clean off.

                         RIDCULLY
          It's not safe to drink it when sweat's
          still condensing on the bottle, though.

He peers at the bottle, and then rubs at it, causing a
glassy, squeaky noise.

                         RIDCULLY
               (brightly)
          On the other hand, if it's a kill-or-
          cure remedy then we are, given that the
          patient is possibly immortal, probably
          on to a winner.

He places a thumb over the cork and shakes the bottle
vigorously.

There is a crash as the Chair of Indefinite Studies
tries to get under the table.

Ridcully cautiously uncorks the bottle. There is a
brief hiss of indrawn air.

The Dean and the Lecturer in
Recent Runes duck down behind
their heavy furniture.

Ridcully allows a few drops
to splash into the beaker.
Nothing happens. He sniffs
suspiciously at the bottle.

                    RIDCULLY
          I wonder if it's
          gone critical yet?

He upturns the sauce and
shakes it. Quite a lot of
sauce goes in and he's
rewarded with a . . . GLOOP.

The wizards begin to stand
up and brush themselves off,
giving one another rather
embarrassed grins.

Ridcully turns the bottle round, peering at it sadly.
Then finally, he tips it up and thumps it hard on the
base.

A trickle of sauce arrives on the lip of the bottle and
glistens there for a moment. Then it begins to form a bead.

                            155

As if drawn by invisible strings, the heads of the wizards turn to look at it.

Susan, drawn by the same invisible strings, also turns to look at it.

As the bead swells and starts to go pear-shaped, the wizards turn and, with a surprising turn of speed for men so wealthy in years and waistline, dive for the floor.

The drop falls. It goes . . . GLOOP. And that is all.

Ridcully, who has been standing like a statue, sags in relief.

                    RIDCULLY
I don't know . . .

He turns away.

                    RIDCULLY
    I wish you fellows would show
some backbone . . .

The FIREBALL erupts from the POTION, lifting Ridcully off his feet, and then rises to the ceiling where it spreads out widely and vanishes with a pop, leaving a perfect chrysanthemum of scorched plaster.

INT. TOOTH FAIRY'S CASTLE/TOOTH FAIRY'S ANTE-ROOM - DAY

Medium Dave is dragging Violet out of the room.

                    TEATIME
    Please just take her out of vocal
    range.

Teatime turns to Mr Brown and indicates towards the door.

                    TEATIME
    Mr Brown. Your big moment.

By the door, Mr Brown is sat on his tool box, which has drawers full of hammers, picks and little chisels in it. He is working on one of the locks. He has a STETHOSCOPE-TYPE DEVICE in his ears as he turns a small dial.

Teatime is stood over his shoulder.

Mr Brown turns the dial one click and then smiles.

As he turns the dial again we hear the sound of bolts falling out of place and . . . a faint hissing sound.

                    TEATIME
          Break me out the real Tooth Fairy.

INT. UNSEEN UNIVERSITY/GREAT HALL - NIGHT

Pure white light fills the room. And there is a sound. TINKLE. TINKLE. FIZZ. (Just like Alka-Seltzers.)

Ridcully picks himself up off the floor.

The beaker gleams. It is filled with a liquid glow which bubbles gently and sends out sparkles like a spinning diamond.

Slowly, with the flickering light casting long shadows on the walls, the wizards gravitate towards the beaker.

Ridcully dips his finger into the liquid. It comes out with one glistening drop on the end.

                    THE DEAN
               Careful,
               Archchancellor.
               What you have there
               might represent
               pure sobriety.

Ridcully pauses with the finger halfway to his lips.

                    BILIOUS
               I'll try it.

Bilious staggers up to the beaker, manages to grip it on the second go, and drinks the lot.

The oh God blinks. The wizards

watch him cautiously.
Remarkably, he seems to be
feeling better.

Bilious smiles briefly at
Susan and promptly COLLAPSES.

The Dean pauses and looks at
Bilious.

> THE DEAN
> You did say he was
> immortal, didn't
> you?

She bends down and slaps
Bilious across the face. Nothing.

The wizards gather round the prostrate oh God.

Susan marches over to one of the laden tables and picks
up a jug of water.

> RIDCULLY
> Did you say he just appeared?

> SUSAN
> Yes. He has no memory of existing
> before appearing at the Hogfather's
> castle.

Ridcully pulls the Verruca Gnome from his pocket.

> RIDCULLY
> Just like this fellow.

> THE DEAN
> Oh don't be ridiculous. Gods and gnomes
> don't just appear en mass for no
> reason.

We hear the sound of a jug of water hitting flesh,
followed by groaning.

A startled Bilious sits up, shakes his head and smiles.

> BILIOUS
> Bring me . . . let's see . . . twenty
> pints of lager, some pepper vodka and a
> bottle of coffee liqueur!

Susan grabs his hand and pulls him over to a bench.

                    SUSAN
          I didn't have you sobered up just so
          you could go on a binge!

                    BILIOUS
          You didn't?

                    SUSAN
          You don't drink.

                    BILIOUS
          I don't? Oh yeah.

                    SUSAN
          I need you to help me.

Ridcully looks at Bilious. His
face flickers as he realises
something.

                    RIDCULLY
          Oh dear. I think I did
          it, didn't I? I said
          something to young
          Stibbons about drinking
          and hangovers, didn't I
          . . . ?

                    THE DEAN
          And you created him
          just like that? I find
          that very hard to
          believe, Mustrum.

The Lecturer in Recent Runes looks at the Dean.

                    LECTURER IN RECENT RUNES
          Good job no one mentioned the Hair Loss
          Fairy then.

The other wizards laugh.

                    THE DEAN
          I am not losing my hair! It is just
          very finely spaced.

                    LECTURER IN RECENT RUNES
          Half on your head and half on your
          hairbrush.

                         THE DEAN
                    (shouting)
          For the last time, I am
          not . . .

          He stops. There is a
          glingleglingleglingle noise.

                         RIDCULLY
          I wish I knew where that
          was coming from.

          Ridcully considers for a minute.

                         RIDCULLY
          We need a bigger brain
          on this.

INT. CHILD'S BEDROOM/ANKH-MORPORK - NIGHT

By the hearth are the usual Hogfather gifts, where
Albert is checking out the quality of the offerings.

At the end of the bed is an empty stocking into which
DEATH is placing a grinning horse.

Hanging from a loop of string above the fireplace are a
number of Hogswatch cards which alternate with paper
sausages. On the mantelpiece, Albert looks at a family
photo, and next to it, one particular card, and sees
that . . .

. . . the jolly Hogfather has been COMPLETELY REPLACED
by the HUMAN father we've seen in the photo.

                         ALBERT
          Master.

DEATH turns.

                         ALBERT
          I think you should take a look at this.

Albert looks worried.

INT. UNSEEN UNIVERSITY/HEX'S ROOM - NIGHT

The door to the room is thrown open and Ridcully
enters. Ponder doesn't even turn round.

                    RIDCULLY
          That thinking engine of yours working,
          Ponder?

                  PONDER STIBBONS
          Hex is resting, Archchancellor.

Ridcully bangs his pipe on HEX's listening tube.

                    RIDCULLY
          CAN YOU HEAR ME IN THERE?

The pen scratches.
          +++ Yes +++

                  PONDER STIBBONS
          You don't have to shout,
          Archchancellor.

                    RIDCULLY
          What's this *glingleglingle* noise all
          about?

Hex's quill quivers into life and Ridcully reads the
text.

                    RIDCULLY
          It says, 'Look at the Dean!   Look at
          the Dean!'

The other wizards turn and stare at the Dean.

Something is moving under his hat. Very carefully, he
reaches up and removes it. A very SMALL GNOME is
pushing a TINY LAWN MOWER across his head. The little
creature stops, looks up, and blinks guiltily in the
light.

                  HAIR LOSS FAIRY
          Is there a problem?

Susan grabs it.

                    SUSAN
          Are you the Hair Loss Fairy?

                  HAIR LOSS FAIRY
          Apparently.

The gnome wriggles in her grip.

The Dean runs his hands desperately through his
hair.

                    THE DEAN
          What have you been doing with my
          hair?

                 HAIR LOSS FAIRY

          Well, some of it I think I have to put on
          hairbrushes, but sometimes I think I weave it
          into little mats to block up the bath with.

                     RIDCULLY
          What do you mean, you think?

                      SUSAN
          Just a minute.

Susan turns to Bilious.

                      SUSAN
          Where exactly were you before I
          found you in the snow?

                     BILIOUS
          Er . . . Anywhere where drink had
          been consumed in beastly
          quantities some time previously,
          you could say.

                     RIDCULLY
          Ah-ha. You were an imminent vital
          force, yes?

                     BILIOUS
          Sounds great. What is that?

                     RIDCULLY
          And when we joked about the Hair
          Loss Fairy it suddenly focused on
          the Dean's head . . .

                      SUSAN
          You're calling things into being.

                     BURSAR
           (cheerfully)
          I personally have always wondered
          if there was an Eater of Socks.
          You know how there's always one
          missing?

The wizards give this some thought. Then they all hear
it . . . *glingleglingleglingle* - the little crinkly
tinkling noise of magic taking place.

The Dean points dramatically skywards.

                    THE DEAN
          To the laundry!

The wizards surge out excitedly, leaving Susan, the oh
God, and . . . Ridcully. He shakes his head.

                    BILIOUS
          Tell me again who these people are.

                    SUSAN
          Some of the cleverest men in the world.

                    BILIOUS
          And I'm sober, am I?

Ridcully and Susan exchange a look . . .

And just at that point a young student wizard crashes
drunkenly through the gable window from the roof and
practically falls over. On his head he wears the
guard's tooth-shaped helmet.

                    RIDCULLY
          What is that ridiculous
          thing on your head?

The student tilts his eyes up to his
headgear.

                    STUDENT WIZARD
               (slurring)
          I dunno, sir.

With which he falls flat on his
face. The helmet rolls off his head
and over to Bilious, who picks it
up and looks inside the helmet.

                    SUSAN
          What? What is it?

He reads a label inside the rim.

                    BILIOUS
          It says here: 'If found please return
          to the Tooth Fairy's castle'.

He looks up, confused.

> RIDCULLY
> Thank goodness the Tooth Fairy already
> exists!

> BILIOUS
> (thinking)
> Tooth Fairy?

> SUSAN
> Oh, you see her around a lot these
> days, or them, rather. It's a sort of
> franchise operation to collect
> children's teeth in exchange for money.

> BILIOUS
> And she has a castle? She sounds great!

Bilious looks at the helmet again.

> BILIOUS
> Actually I do remember one thing.

Susan turns towards him.

> BILIOUS
> Just when I appeared at the Hogfather's
> house there was a drunken little fellow
> in a pointy hat. I thought it was just
> the drink talking, but he did mention
> something about the . . .

INT. CASTLE OF BONES/THRONE ROOM – NIGHT

FLASHBACK to the Pixie Helper, who is now in serious
mode.

> PIXIE HELPER
> . . . permanent end of perpetual
> servitude for the little helpers of all
> fantasy personifications . . .

INT. UNSEEN UNIVERSITY/HEX'S ROOM – NIGHT

> RIDCULLY
> He must have been very drunk.

> BILIOUS
> . . . including the Tooth Fairy . . .

Ridcully takes the helmet from Bilious, hurries over to the student and slaps him awake.

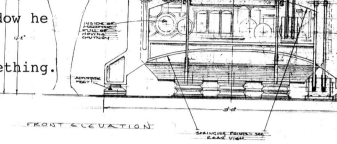

> RIDCULLY
> Where did you find this?

The student groggily points towards the window he came in through.

Susan looks at Ridcully. At last, maybe something.

They hurry to the window.

EXT. UNSEEN UNIVERSITY/ROOF - NIGHT

Susan, Ridcully and Bilious all poke their heads out of the small gable window and look across the roof.

A dead Tooth Fairy's guard is slumped in the snow.

INT. UNSEEN UNIVERSITY/HEX'S ROOM - NIGHT

The group come back in. Ridcully hurries over to Hex.

Susan kisses Bilious on the forehead.

> SUSAN
> I am so glad you're sober!

Ridcully leans into Hex's speaking tube . . .

> RIDCULLY
> Tell us the geographical location of
> the Tooth Fairy's castle.

INT. TOOTH FAIRY'S CASTLE/TOOTH FAIRY'S ANTE-ROOM - DAY

Mr Brown is concentrating hard on the lock to the door, until there is a click. He looks back at the gang and a smile crosses his face.

Medium Dave and Chickenwire inch forward to see . . .

There is a rush of air releasing, as if a seal has been broken that blows the locksmith's hair back and . . .

. . . shadows rush across his face.

                    MR BROWN (O.C.)
            (terrified)
        No!

INT. CHILD'S BEDROOM/ANKH-MORPORK - NIGHT

Albert is sat on the bed looking miserably at the pork
pie.

                    ALBERT
            It's all been a waste of time. They're
            winnin', master. I'm knackerin' my
            kidneys and cloggin' my arteries with
            pork jelly for nothin'.

He takes a sad bite.

                    ALBERT
            Well, not quite nothin'.

He looks closer at the pork pie.

                    ALBERT
            And to top it all there is a worm in
            this one!

                    DEATH
            IT'S FAT.

                    ALBERT
            I know it's fat, it's eaten all the
            meat!

                    DEATH
            DO I DETECT A NOTE OF UNSEASONAL
            GRUMPINESS? NO SUGAR PIGGYWIGGY FOR
            YOU, ALBERT.

                    ALBERT
            I don't want any present, master.
            Except maybe to wake up and find it's
            all back to normal. Look, you know it
            always goes wrong when you start
            changing things.

He puts the last bit of tobacco into a roll-up.

                    DEATH
            BUT THE HOGFATHER CAN CHANGE THINGS.
            LITTLE MIRACLES ALL OVER THE PLACE,
            WITH MANY A MERRY HO, HO, HO. TEACHING

PEOPLE THE REAL MEANING OF
HOGSWATCH, ALBERT.

                    ALBERT
          It's all about the sun,
          master. White snow and red
          blood and the sun. Always
          has been.

                    DEATH
          VERY WELL, THEN. THE
          HOGFATHER WILL TEACH PEOPLE
          THE REAL REAL MEANING OF
          HOGSWATCH.

EXT. SKY – NIGHT

DEATH is deep in thought.

                    DEATH
          I LIKE THIS JOB.

Albert spits over the side of the sleigh and
as he does fails to see the tobacco blow out
of the cigarette paper.

                    ALBERT
          Oh dear, oh dear, oh
          dear . . .

Finally Albert lights the cigarette. He
smiles. It bursts into flames.

                    DEATH
          EXCUSE ME . . .

DEATH reaches into his robe and pulls out a
Lifetimer. He looks at the dwindling sand
and taps the glass with a finger.

                    DEATH
          YES. THIS WILL SHOW
          THEM . . .

And the sleigh jerks down once more.

EXT. MONEY TRAP LANE/ANKH MORPORK – NIGHT

DEATH and Albert in the sleigh swerve around

at the end of the street.

                    ALBERT
          But . . . little match girls dying in
          the snow is part of what the Hogswatch
          spirit is all about, master. It makes
          them feel happy and grateful for what
          they've got, see.

                    DEATH
          I KNOW WHAT THE SPIRIT OF HOGSWATCH IS,
          ALBERT.

Albert frowns. They have reached the spot.

DEATH looks down at the shape under the falling snow.
Then he sets the Lifetimer on the air and touches it
with a finger. A spark flashes across.

                    ALBERT
             (feeling wretched)
          You ain't really allowed to
          do that.

                    DEATH
          THE HOGFATHER CAN. THE
          HOGFATHER GIVES PRESENTS.
          THERE'S NO BETTER PRESENT
          THAN A FUTURE.

DEATH scoops up the girl and
strides to the end of the alley,
steps out into the street and
accosts two figures who are
tramping through the drifts.

                    DEATH
             (commanding)
          TAKE HER SOMEWHERE
          WARM AND GIVE HER A
          GOOD DINNER.

He pushes the bundle into
the arms of one of them.

                    DEATH
          AND I MAY WELL BE
          CHECKING UP LATER.

Then he turns and disappears into the swirling
snow.

Constable Visit looks down at the little girl in his arms, pulls aside the blanket and then looks at Corporal Nobbs.

                    CORPORAL NOBBS
          Looks like we've been
          chosen to do a bit of
          charity.

                    CONSTABLE VISIT
          I don't call it very
          charitable, just
          dumping someone on
          people like this.

                    CORPORAL NOBBS
          I dunno. Some people wouldn't know the
          real meaning of Hogswatch if it came up
          and clocked 'em in the gob.

They trudge off into the snow anyway.

MOMENTS LATER:

. . . at the other end of the alley the Auditors
materialise from the mists of the snow. They flutter
over the match girl-shaped hole in the snow and look
around confused.

                    AUDITOR 2
          He is not authorised to do that.

                    AUDITOR 3
          This is an alarming deviation.

                    AUDITOR 2
          Definitively off-message.

                    AUDITOR 1
          It must not be allowed to compromise a
          better, simpler future.

                    AUDITOR 4
          Or it will surely end in complications.

                    AUDITOR 3
            (panicking)
          Ah yes, but for whom?

                    AUDITOR 2
          Who.

                              AUDITOR 3
                    It's whom, definitely.

The robes all look at each other. Whom . . . exactly.

                              AUDITOR 2
                    At least the Assassin has stuck
                    strictly to his brief.

                              AUDITOR 4
                    Actually . . . where is the Assassin?

There is a flutter of concern . . .

INT. TOOTH FAIRY'S CASTLE/TOOTH FAIRY'S ANTE-ROOM – DAY

Teatime is right in Mr Brown's face. The locksmith is
stood back from the door. He looks white.

                              TEATIME
                    I was told you were the best locksmith
                    in the city.

Mr Sideney is stood like a petrified statue . . . with
his thumb in his mouth.

Medium Dave is trying to get a crowbar into the gap at
the side of the door. He gets it in a little way, puts
his weight against it but it won't hold and he lurches
backwards.

Teatime stares at Mr Brown with that gaze.

The locksmith looks away as a SHADOW ripples across his
face and he lays down his pick.

Mr Brown looks flustered.

                              MR BROWN
                    Well, yes. But locks don't generally
                    alter 'emselves while you're working on
                    'em, that's what I'm saying.

                              TEATIME
                    Are you the best or not?

Mr Brown reluctantly goes back to his work.

                              TEATIME
                    Mr Sideney?

Teatime turns. But Sideney has gone . . .

Medium Dave turns. So has Chickenwire . . .

The Assassin and Dave leave the room.

INT. TOOTH FAIRY'S CASTLE/FOOT OF TOWER - DAY

Banjo is sat in a hand-cart, swinging his feet
contentedly looking up at the teeth where Sideney is
stood.

The wizard looks up to the top of the tower to see if
anyone's looking and then hurries over to Banjo.

> MR SIDENEY
> Banjo, I'm getting out of here. There's
> something wrong with this place.

> BANJO
> (smiling)
> I made a big pile.

> MR SIDENEY

> Do you want to come with me?

> BANJO
> It's pretty here.

Sideney shrugs, puts his pointy hat on and starts to
move towards the door.

> TEATIME (O.C.)
> Mr Sideney.

Sideney stops. Teatime is stood at the door. The
wizard's shoulders slump.

INT. UNSEEN UNIVERSITY/LAUNDRY ENGINE ROOM - NIGHT

Ridcully enters. It is utter pandemonium.

The Dean is trying to grab the Hair Loss Fairy from
under his hat.

The wizards are gathered round something we can't see.

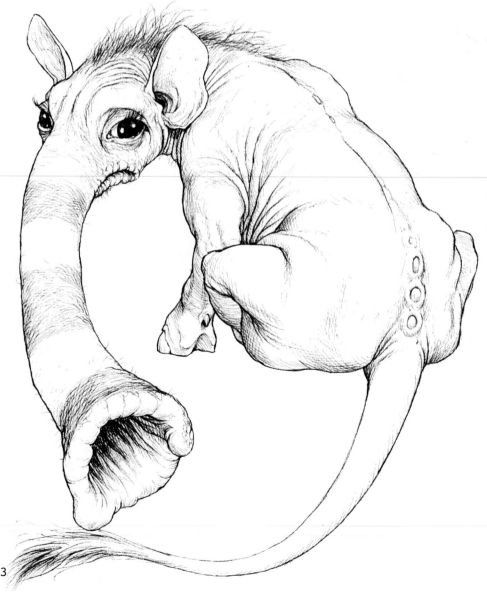

CHAIR OF INDEFINITE STUDIES
(uncertainly)
Shoo?!

A striped proboscis sucks the Chair of Indefinite
Studies' boot off his foot.

The boot flies past his head.

The EATER OF SOCKS looks like a very SMALL ELEPHANT
with a very wide, flared trunk. It sucks the sock off
the wizard's foot, stuffs it in its mouth.

EATER OF SOCKS
. . . grnf, grnf . . .

The wizard makes a grab for it.

The wizards chase the Sock Eater
behind one of the boilers.

The Verruca Gnome chases the
Chair of Indefinite Studies'
bare feet. The wizard tries
to put his foot into a big
WASHING ENGINE in an attempt
to keep it away from the
creature.

RIDCULLY
We've got to get
this sorted out.
Can't have creatures
just popping into
existence because
someone's thought
about them. It's
unhygienic.

Ridcully pulls open a
drawer in his hat and
extracts his pipe and a
pouch of herbal tobacco.

He strikes a match on the
side of the washing engine
and as he does . . .

. . . . the Eater of Socks
knocks Ridcully head over
heels.

INT. UNSEEN UNIVERSITY/CORRIDOR - NIGHT

Susan strides fast down the corridor. Bilious is running to try to catch her.

> BILIOUS
> Now I'm feeling normal, can I come with you?

He catches up with Susan.

> SUSAN
> This is not a normal situation. Look . . .

Susan takes a big breath.

> SUSAN
> I think I'd better tell you . . . My grandfather is DEATH.

> BILIOUS
> Oh, I'm sorry to hear that.

> SUSAN
> DEATH. You know . . . DEATH? The robes, the . . . scythe, white horse, bones . . . DEATH. But at the moment he's acting rather strange.

> BILIOUS
> I just want to make sure I've got this clear. You think your grandfather is Death and you think he's acting strange?

Bilious looks at her. Susan's eyes seem to have dark eye shadow around them. She hesitates, then as if by rote . . .

> SUSAN
> Look, DEATH adopted my mother, he took on a human apprentice, they fell in love and I'm the result.

> BILIOUS
> This is fascinating.

> SUSAN
> Let's just say I picked up a few strange genetic knacks along the way.

Susan walks through a big door. Bilious bumps into it.

EXT. UNSEEN UNIVERSITY/OCTANGLE - NIGHT

Susan emerges from the building and looks up as the University CLOCK chimes TWO O'CLOCK.

Binky is waiting in the Octangle. Susan goes over to him.

Behind her Bilious finally heaves the door open.

Susan reaches the horse.

Susan pulls herself up.

Bilious runs after her.

Susan reaches under her coat. Her wrist moves. A sparkling blue line flashes in the air, for a moment outlining an edge too thin to be seen. Susan seems to be holding a sword hilt with no blade.

The oh God backs away.

>   BILIOUS
>   Now that looks dangerous.

Susan sheathes the sword.

>   SUSAN
>   I hope so.

Binky starts to trot but, just before he's about to leave the ground, Bilious jumps up behind her on the horse.

Susan groans and looks back.

>   SUSAN
>   Finding the Tooth Fairy could be
>   dangerous. Would you be any good in a
>   fight?

>   BILIOUS
>   Yes. I could be sick on people.

And with that, Binky leaps into the air.

INT. UNSEEN UNIVERSITY/HEX'S ROOM - NIGHT

Ridcully shouts into Hex's listening tube.

> RIDCULLY
> So what's this Implied Creation, then?

Hex's quill pen scratches away . . .

> *+++ Humans Have Always Ascribed Random, Seasonal, Natural Or Inexplicable Actions To Human-Shaped Entities. Such Examples Are The Hogfather, The Tooth Fairy And Death +++*

Ridcully looks up from the paper and strokes his beard.

> RIDCULLY
> All right, but I'm damn sure there's never been an Eater of Socks or an oh God of Hangovers.

Ponder Stibbons is making notes.

> PONDER STIBBONS
> I think it works like this. What we're getting is the personification of forces, just like Hex said.

> RIDCULLY
> Bit like the Hogfather. When you're a kiddie, he's as good an explanation of where the presents come from as any, right?

Ponder shrugs a sort of agreement.

> RIDCULLY
> But why's it happening now?

Ridcully and Ponder look at Hex in unison.

The sound of Hex's quill as it scrabbles across the paper is like a frantic spider trapped in a matchbox, and then it comes to a rest.

> *+++ Belief's Causing New Creatures To Appear +++*

> RIDCULLY
> Yes. Yes, you could put it like that.

178

+++ There's A Finite Quantity Of Belief In The Universe +++

Ridcully looks at Ponder. He shrugs.

                    RIDCULLY
Certainly people can only believe in so
many things.

+++ It Follows That If A Major Focus Of Belief Is Removed, There Will Be Spare Belief +++

Ridcully stares at the words.

                    RIDCULLY
All right, then, so what are people not
believing in all of a sudden?

+++ Out Of Cheese Error +++ MELON MELON MELON +++ Redo From Start +++

                 PONDER STIBBONS
It's Hogswatch. I suppose the Hogfather
is around, isn't he?

INT. UNSEEN UNIVERSITY/LIBRARY - NIGHT

The wizards are sat in the library . . . in the dark.
We can just about make out the shiny bits on their
hats.

                 PONDER STIBBONS
I'm waiting for the Hogfather. I'm in
the dark waiting for the Hogfather. Me.
A believer in Natural Philosophy. I can
find the square root of 27.4 in my
head. I shouldn't be doing this. It's
not as if I've hung a stocking up.
There'd be some point if . . .

He sits rigid for a moment, and then pulls off his
pointy sandal and rolls down a sock.

EXT. A CHILD'S SKY - NIGHT

Binky flies down through white clouds to reveal . . .
swirls. The horse gallops easily through them, except
that he does not seem to move. He might be hanging in
the air. The swirls vanish.

The oh God risks a look down.

> BILIOUS
> (weakly)
> Oh me.

There is greenery below. If green could be a primary colour, this is it. And there's a blue wiggly thing . . .

Above the green there is just the sun, floating above the land. It is yellow . . . buttercup yellow.

Binky lands on the grass beside the river. Or at least on the green. Susan slides off, and looks down at the vivid blue of the water.

There are orange fish in it. They are made of two curved lines and a dot and a triangular tail. She kneels down and dips her hand in. What pours through her fingers is liquid blue. A smile crosses her face, as if she now knows where she is.

> SUSAN
> This is a child's painting.

The oh God jumps down from Binky.

> SUSAN
> Twyla paints like that. I painted like that. Grandfather saved some of my draw—

She stops.

> SUSAN
> Come on, let's find the house.

> BILIOUS
> (moaning)
> What house?

> SUSAN
> There's always a house . . .

Susan pulls Bilious along and suddenly they are out of the trees. There, by a bend in the river, is the HOUSE.

It doesn't look very big. There are four windows and a door. Corkscrew smoke curls out of the chimney.

Susan hesitates and then they start to walk towards it . . .

INT. UNSEEN UNIVERSITY/LIBRARY - NIGHT

Ridcully and Ponder are still waiting in the dark for
the Hogfather.

> RIDCULLY
> Would he deliver to apes earlier than
> humans?

> PONDER STIBBONS
> Interesting point, sir. Possibly
> you're referring to my theory that
> humans may have in fact descended
> from apes, of course. A bold
> hypothesis which, if the Grants
> Committee could just see their way
> clear to letting me hire a boat and
> sail around to the Islands of . . .

> RIDCULLY
> I just thought he might deliver
> alphabetically.

There is a patter of soot in the cold
fireplace. Something lands in the ashes.

The two wizards stand quietly in the
darkness.

The scarcely discernible figure picks itself
up. There is a rustle of paper.

> DEATH (O.C.)
> LET ME SEE NOW.

There is a click as Ridcully's pipe falls out of his
mouth.

INT. TOOTH FAIRY'S CASTLE/TOOTH FAIRY'S ANTE-ROOM - DAY

Mr Brown is still working at one of the locks.

> TEATIME
> I believe there are seven locks?

> MR BROWN
> Yes, but . . . they're half magic and
> half real and half not there . . . I
> mean . . . there's parts of them that
> don't exist all the time . . .

TEATIME
And I thought you could open any lock
anyone ever made.

MR BROWN
(sharply)
Made by humans. And most dwarfs. I
dunno what made these. You never said
anything about magic.

The locksmith gives the lock a frustrated bang with his
fist and then turns to face Teatime. There is a hissing
sound from the lock.

TEATIME
That's a shame. Then really I have no
more need of your services. You may as
well go back home.

Mr Brown starts putting things back into his tool bag.

MR BROWN
What about my money?

TEATIME
Of course, you should get what you
deserve. Banjo?

Banjo lumbers forward, and then stops.

Mr Brown's hand comes out of the bag holding a crowbar.

MR BROWN
You must think I was born yesterday, Mr
Teacup. I'm leaving, right? With what's
coming to me. And you ain't stopping
me. And Banjo
certainly ain't. I
knew his old Ma back
in the good old days.

Mr Brown glares at Teatime,
flourishing the crowbar.

MR BROWN
You think you're
nasty? You think
you're mean? Ma
Lilywhite'd tear your
ears off and spit 'em
in your eye, you cocky
little devil.

Banjo lifts Mr Brown up by the crowbar so that his feet
come out of his boots. He struggles in mid-air.

> MR BROWN
> I remembers you when you was little,
> Banjo, I used to sit you on my knees
> . . .

> TEATIME
> Banjo!

From the crack around the door DARK SHADOWS seep out
and then rush across the walls as we hear the sounds of
Mr Brown struggling.

INT. UNSEEN UNIVERSITY/LIBRARY - NIGHT

Ridcully picks up his pipe.

> RIDCULLY
> Who the hell are you?

DEATH backs away.

The wizards are waiting for a response from
DEATH.

> DEATH
> I'M THE HOGFATHER, OF COURSE. ER.
> HO. HO. HO.

Ridcully looks closer.

> RIDCULLY
> You look extremely thin in the face!

> DEATH
> I'M . . . I AM A BIT ILL.

> RIDCULLY
> Terminally, I should say.

Ridcully grabs the beard. There is a twang
as the string gives way.

> RIDCULLY
> It's a false beard!

> DEATH
> (desperately)
> NO IT'S NOT.

183

RIDCULLY

Here's the hooks for
the ears, which must
have given you a bit
of trouble, I must
say!

Ridcully flourishes the
incriminating evidence and
prods DEATH in the cushion
with it.

Ponder looks horrified.

INT. TOOTH FAIRY'S CASTLE/ROOM - NIGHT

Medium Dave comes into the room.
Chickenwire is hiding in a corner.

MEDIUM DAVE

There you are.

CHICKENWIRE

Where are all these shadows coming
from? They gives me the creeps. It's
all your fault.

MEDIUM DAVE

Oh, yeah? So it wasn't you who said,
wow, ten thousand dollars, count me in?

CHICKENWIRE

I didn't know there was going to be all
this creepy stuff! I want to go home!

MEDIUM DAVE

Blimey, it's like dealing with a chil—

Then, high above them . . . a scream. It goes on for a
while and seems to be getting nearer. Then it stops and
is replaced by a rush of thumping and an occasional
sound like a coconut being bounced on a stone floor.

Medium Dave opens the door . . . just in time to see
the body of Mr Brown the locksmith tumble past, moving
quite fast and not at all neatly.

Mr Brown's bag of tools somersault around the curve of
the stairs. It splits and there is a jangle as crowbars
and lockpicks bounce out and follow their late owner.

Medium Dave looks up. Two turns of stairs above him, on the opposite side of the huge shaft, Banjo is watching him.

> MEDIUM DAVE
> Er . . . poor guy must've slipped.

> CHICKENWIRE
> Oh, yeah . . . slipped.

He looks up too. There are shadows, moving across the stone. In the stone.

I/E. TOOTH FAIRY'S CASTLE/ENTRANCE HALL - DAY

As Susan and Bilious get closer we realise that the child's house is actually quite small. At the door Susan turns the doorknob and crouches down to go in.

Inside, the oh God gasps. The building is enormous.

The staircases start opposite one another in what is now a big round tower, its ceiling lost in the haze. The spirals circle into infinity.

Susan's eyes go to a large conical heap in the middle of the floor. It is white and glistens in the cool light that shines down from the mists.

> SUSAN
> It's teeth.

> BILIOUS
> (looking faint)
> And I should be scared?

> SUSAN
> There's nothing that scary about teeth.

From Susan's face as she looks at, it's clear she doesn't mean it.

The heap is very horrible indeed.

> BILIOUS
> Did I say I was scared? I must just be hung-over again . . .

Susan advances on the heap, moving warily.

185

They are small teeth. Children's teeth. A chalk mark
has been drawn around the obscene heap.

                    SUSAN
          (quietly)
          This isn't right. All that effort to
          get the teeth, and then just to dump
          them like this? No . . .

She stares down at the chalk marks.

                    BILIOUS
          They're only teeth.

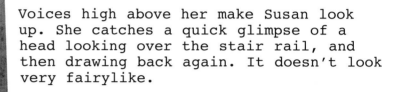

Voices high above her make Susan look
up. She catches a quick glimpse of a
head looking over the stair rail, and
then drawing back again. It doesn't look
very fairylike.

She glances back at the circle of chalk
around the teeth.

There are a few symbols scrawled around
the circle.

                    SUSAN
          Oh, no . . . Surely no one
          would try to . . .

                    BILIOUS
          What's it for?

                    SUSAN
          (sighing)
          It's such old magic it isn't
          even magic any more. If you've
          got a piece of someone's hair,
          or a nail clipping, or a
          tooth, you can control them. Oh
          my, don't tell me someone's . . .

The oh God tries to focus just as . . . someone shouts,
someone up in the whiteness. A shadow flitters across
the wall.

                    SUSAN
          This place is alive.

A body rolls down the stairs nearest her, then tumbles
across the white marble and slides to a boneless halt.
It's MR BROWN.

Then, as she hurries towards the body, it fades away, leaving nothing behind but a smear of blood.

> SUSAN
> And it's protecting itself.

A *jingle* noise makes her look back up the stairs. Spinning over and over, a CROWBAR bounds over the last steps and lands point first, staying upright and vibrating.

Susan stops in her tracks.

INT. TOOTH FAIRY'S CASTLE/TOOTH FAIRY'S ANTE-ROOM - NIGHT

Chickenwire reaches the top of the stairs, panting.

> CHICKENWIRE
> (wheezing)
> There's people down there, Mister Teatime!

Teatime doesn't take his eyes off the wizard.

> TEATIME
> Well? Just . . . do away with them.

> CHICKENWIRE
> Er . . . one of them's a girl, sir.

Teatime still doesn't look round. He waves a hand vaguely.

> TEATIME
> Then do away with them politely.

Teatime turns to Sideney.

> TEATIME
> Keep going . . . quicker.

Sideney turns quickly back to his work.

Chickenwire stands there for a moment, and then hurries off.

INT. TOOTH FAIRY'S CASTLE/STAIRS - DAY

Chickenwire scurries down the stairs. He hears a creak, as of an ancient wooden door. He goes pale. The look on his face is as if he has had some terrible memory. He gives a little yelp and starts to take the stairs four at a time.

In the hollows and corners, the shadows grow darker.

INT. TOOTH FAIRY'S CASTLE/LOWER STAIRS - DAY

Susan runs up a flight of stairs, dragging the oh God behind her.

INT. TOOTH FAIRY'S CASTLE/BOTTOM OF TOWER - NIGHT

A trembling Chickenwire reaches the bottom of the tower and heads straight for the door until . . .

. . . a hand grabs him. It's Medium Dave.

> CHICKENWIRE
> Let me out! It's after me!

Medium Dave slaps him across the face.

> MEDIUM DAVE
> Pull yourself together! Look around!
> Nothing's chasing you!

Chickenwire looks back up the stairs. There is nothing there. He looks at his feet.

> CHICKENWIRE
> (muttering)
> I thought it was the wardrobe.

> MEDIUM DAVE
> What wardrobe?

> CHICKENWIRE
> Oh, when I was a kid . . .

Chickenwire waves his arms vaguely.

> CHICKENWIRE
> We had this big ole wardrobe. It had

this . . . this . . . on the door
there was this . . . sort of . . .
face an' at night . . .

Chickenwire's voice goes as quiet as a vole in a
dungeon.

> CHICKENWIRE
> . . . it whispered things.

Medium Dave squints upwards.

> MEDIUM DAVE
> Who's that moving up there?

INT. TOOTH FAIRY'S CASTLE/CORRIDOR - NIGHT

Susan darts off the stairs and drags the oh God along a
corridor lined with white doors.

> SUSAN
> I think they saw us. And if they're
> tooth fairies there's been a really
> stupid Equal Opportunities policy . . .

She pushes open a door.

INT. TOOTH FAIRY'S CASTLE/MONEY ROOM - DAY

Susan enters and sees the open safe doors and piles of
title deeds left scattered on the floor.

She crosses the passage to another room . . .

INT. TOOTH FAIRY'S CASTLE/PASSAGEWAY - DAY

Medium Dave and Chickenwire run down the passage until
they come to a split of ways.

> MEDIUM DAVE
> You go that way, I'll . . .

> CHICKENWIRE
> (terrified)
> Why don't we stick together?

> MEDIUM DAVE
> What's got into you?

He walks off.

Chickenwire peers down the other passage. There aren't many doors down there. It isn't very long. He starts to walk down it. There is a distant creaking sound behind him.

INT. TOOTH FAIRY'S CASTLE/DISPLAY CASE ROOM 3 – DAY

There are no windows to the room, but it's lit perfectly well by the white walls themselves. Susan and Bilious walk down the middle of the room alongside something like display cases with their lids gaping open. Bits of card litter the floor.

A scream of shock. Susan turns sharply towards the door.

> BILIOUS
> What was that?

> SUSAN
> It's finding their nightmares.

Susan throws open the door.

INT. TOOTH FAIRY'S CASTLE/STAIRS – DAY

Susan and Bilious manage another flight and open another door.

INT. TOOTH FAIRY'S CASTLE/CORRIDOR – DAY

Susan and Bilious enter the corridor. Susan stops.

> SUSAN
> This is a children's place. The rules are what children believe.

> BILIOUS
> Well, that's a relief.

> SUSAN
> (ominously)
> You think so? You were never a child. And it's possible to die here. My Grandfather doesn't figure in a child's world.

190

                    BILIOUS
That man who fell down the stairs
looked pretty dead to me.

                     SUSAN
Oh, you die. But not here. You . . .
let's see . . . yes . . . you go
somewhere else. Away.

                  VOICE (O.C.)
Er . . . hello?

The voice comes from the door they are passing. Susan
and Bilious look at each other.

INT. TOOTH FAIRY'S CASTLE/DISPLAY CASE
ROOM 1 - DAY

Susan and Bilious hurry into the room.

Sitting on the floor and tied to the leg of a
white display case, is Violet. She looks up in
apprehension . . .

Susan hurries over and rips off the gag . . .

                    VIOLET
Aren't you . . . ?

                    SUSAN
Yes, yes and when you came for
Twyla's last tooth you were so
shocked that I could see you . . .

                    VIOLET
   (Interrupts)
Yes, and you . . .

Susan fumbles with the ropes. Violet keeps talking.

                    SUSAN
   (Interrupts)
I don't think we've got a lot of time.

                   BILIOUS
Is this the Tooth Fairy?

                    SUSAN
A Tooth Fairy.

The oh God looks at Violet and tries to push his lank
hair into place. He has the glazed look of one smitten.

                    BILIOUS
          Do you drink at all?

Violet looks confused, but unable to take her doe eyes
from Bilious.

                    VIOLET
            No, I don't!

The oh God raises his eyebrows at Susan.

                    BILIOUS
          Not touch alcohol at all?

                    VIOLET
          Never! My dad's very strict about
          that sort of thing!

Now Bilious looks really besotted.

                    BILIOUS
          Nice castle.

After a moment Susan feels forced to wave a
hand across their locked gaze.

                    SUSAN
          Can we get on?

Their gaze breaks reluctantly. The oh God
helps her on to her feet.

                    SUSAN
            Good. Who brought you here,
          Violet?

                    VIOLET
          I don't know! But he's dressed like an
          Assassin.

Susan looks dubiously at the two of them.

                    SUSAN
          OK. You stay here while I find him . . .

                    BILIOUS
          . . . And I'll look after Violet.

Susan leaves the room.

INT. UNSEEN UNIVERSITY/LIBRARY - NIGHT

The library clock strikes FOUR O'CLOCK.

Ridcully steps closer to DEATH.

> RIDCULLY
> So what's happened to the other
> fellow?

DEATH ponders for a moment.

> DEATH
> WELL . . .

The wizards are gathered around DEATH.

> DEATH
> THE HOGFATHER HAS ENEMIES.

> RIDCULLY
> What did he do? Miss a chimney?

DEATH looks down at them and thrums his
fingers on his scythe.

INT. TOOTH FAIRY'S CASTLE/TOOTH FAIRY'S ANTE-ROOM - DAY

Teatime watches over Sideney as he puts a green filter
over his lantern and presses down on the lock with a
small silver rod that has an emerald set on its tip. A
piece of the lock moves. There is a whirring from
inside the door and something goes click. He sags with
relief.

> MR SIDENEY
> I, er, think that's the fourth lock.

> TEATIME
> I commend your expertise. And the
> others?

Sideney looks up nervously at the silent bulk of Banjo,
and licks his lips. There is a hissing sound and the
wizard looks back down.

A wisp of vapour oozes from the crack between the door
and the frame.

MR SIDENEY
Do you know exactly what's in here,
Mister Teh-ah-time-eh?

TEATIME
Logically, if you are the guardian of
children's beliefs and this is your
castle and I come across as securely
locked a door as this, then not to
thoroughly investigate would . . .

Teatime searches carefully for the word . . .

TEATIME
. . . lack elegance.

Sideney looks up, fear in his eyes.

MR SIDENEY
What was that? That sound . . .

TEATIME
What sound?

MR SIDENEY
It sounded . . . like all scissors
scraping . . .

The wizard's thumb moves slowly to his
mouth.

INT. TOOTH FAIRY'S CASTLE/CORRIDOR - DAY

Violet and the oh God amble down the
stairs.

VIOLET
What sort of Godding do you do?

Violet is round-eyed with fascination.

Bilious is smitten. But suddenly someone is behind him
holding a WIRE tight to his throat.

CHICKENWIRE
What's this? Lover's Lane?

VIOLET
You leave him alone, you! He's a god!

Bilious swallows, gasping. But out of the corner of his eye he can see shadows moving very fast across the walls.

Chickenwire is looking jittery.

                    CHICKENWIRE
          Dear me, out of thunderbolts, are we?
          Well, y'know, I've never . . .

There is a creak.

Chickenwire's face is a few inches from Bilious. The thief's eyes roll. His lips say 'nur . . .' like a child.

Bilious risks stepping back. Chickenwire's grip loosens on the wire. He stands there, trembling slightly. The oh God looks up at the thing on the landing above.

It is just a wardrobe. Dark oak, a bit of fancy woodwork glued on.

Chickenwire's garrotte falls to the floor.

He takes a step backwards up the stairs, but very slowly, and then spins round.

Bilious looks on in shocked amazement.

Chickenwire just revolves, as if some giant hand has been placed on his head and twisted a hundred and eighty degrees. He is level with the lock on the wardrobe door.

The lock has decoration around the keyhole which at first looks like flowers and leaves, but looked at in the right way there is a face . . .

. . . and Chickenwire is looking at it in exactly the right way . . .

The doors of the wardrobe swing open.

                    BILIOUS
          What's the matter?

Chickenwire manages to thrust out his arms and grab the sides and, for a moment, he stands quite still.

                    BILIOUS
          It's just a wardrobe, isn't it?

In one sudden movement Chickenwire is pulled into the wardrobe and the doors slam shut.

The little brass key turns in the lock with a click.

The oh God runs up the steps to the wardrobe. He turns the key and opens the doors.

> VIOLET
> I don't want to see! I don't want to see!

Violet looks over his shoulder.

Bilious reaches down and picks up a pair of boots that stand neatly in the middle of the wardrobe's floor.

Then he puts them back carefully and walks around the wardrobe. It is plywood. He looks closer.

The words *Dratley and Sons, Phedre Road, Ankh-Morpork* are stamped in one corner in faded ink.

INT. UNSEEN UNIVERSITY/LIBRARY – NIGHT

DEATH steeples his long bony fingers in front of him.

> DEATH
> HAVE YOU EVER HEARD OF THE AUDITORS?

> RIDCULLY
> I suppose the Bursar might have done . . .

> DEATH
> NOT AUDITORS OF MONEY. AUDITORS OF REALITY. THEY ARE THE CIVIL SERVICE OF EVERYTHING.

Ridcully grimaces at the thought.

> RIDCULLY
> And they want to get rid of us?

> DEATH
> THEY WANT HUMANS TO BE . . . LESS . . . CREATIVE. THE HOGFATHER IS A SYMBOL OF THIS . . .

DEATH snaps his fingers, causing
echoes to bounce off the walls.

> DEATH
> . . . STRANGE THINKING. THEY
> HATE THE WAY HUMANS MAKE UP
> STORIES ABOUT THE UNIVERSE.

> RIDCULLY
> I can't imagine why. Anyway,
> why're you doing the job?

> DEATH
> SOMEONE MUST. IT IS VITALLY
> IMPORTANT. BEFORE DAWN, THERE
> MUST BE ENOUGH BELIEF IN THE
> HOGFATHER.

> RIDCULLY
> Why?

> DEATH
> SO THAT THE SUN WILL COME UP.

The wizards gawp at him.

> DEATH
> I SELDOM JOKE.

They gather their thoughts.

> PONDER STIBBONS
> Hex was right, Archchancellor.

> DEATH
> HEX? WHO IS HEX?

> PONDER STIBBONS
> Er . . . He is the biggest thinker in
> the world.

DEATH drums the tips of his fingers together,
thoughtfully.

> DEATH
> I WOULD LIKE TO MEET THIS MR HEX.

At which point there is a scream of horror from a
cupboard.

The wizards hurry over and open it. The reason for the
scream is lying on the floor. It's Chickenwire's dead body.

Ridcully pushes his way through the crowd.

                    RIDCULLY
          Ye gods.

The face of the corpse looks as though it died of
fright.

Ridcully looks at the feet. It has no boots on.

The Dean takes a small glass cube from his pocket and
runs it over the corpse.

                    THE DEAN
          Quite a large thaumic reading,
          gentlemen. I think he got here by
          magic.

Ridcully looks around for DEATH . . . who is not there.

INT. UNSEEN UNIVERSITY/HEX'S ROOM – NIGHT

DEATH looks up at Hex. The points of blue light in his
sockets flare.

                    DEATH
          THEY SAY YOU ARE THE BIGGEST THINKER IN
          THE WORLD. BUT DO YOU ALSO BELIEVE?

HEX scribbles:

     +++ Yes +++

                    DEATH
          EXTEND LOGICALLY THE RESULT OF THE
          HUMAN RACE CEASING TO BELIEVE IN THE
          HOGFATHER. WILL THE SUN COME UP?
          ANSWER.

The wheels spin. The ants run. The mouse squeaks. An
eggtimer comes down on a spring. It bounces aimlessly
for a while, and then jerks back up again.

HEX writes:

     +++ The Sun Will Not Come Up +++

                    DEATH
          CORRECT. HOW MAY THIS BE PREVENTED?
          ANSWER.

+++ Regular and Consistent Belief +++

                DEATH
GOOD. I HAVE A TASK FOR YOU, THINKING
ENGINE. BELIEVE IN THE HOGFATHER.

+++ Yes +++

                DEATH
DO YOU BELIEVE? ANSWER.

+++ Yes +++

                DEATH
DO . . . YOU . . . BELIEVE? ANSWER.

+++ YES +++

There is a change in the ill-assembled heap of pipes
and tubes that is Hex. The big wheel creaks into a new
position. From the other side of the wall comes the hum
of busy bees.

                DEATH
  GOOD.

DEATH turns to leave the room, but stops when Hex
begins to write furiously. He goes back and looks at
the emerging paper.

*+++ Dear Hogfather, For Hogswatch I
Want . . . +++*

                DEATH
  OH, NO.

DEATH waits until the pen has stopped and picks up the
paper. He reads the list, groans and then rummages in
his sack.

                DEATH
LET ME SEE . . . HOW OLD ARE YOU?

DEATH leans in to the workings.

                DEATH
AND HAVE YOU BEEN NAUGHTY . . . OR
NICE?

INT. TOOTH FAIRY'S CASTLE/STAIRS BY TF'S ANTE-ROOM – DAY

Susan creeps up the stairs, one hand on the hilt of the sword.

She can hear voices above her. She peers over the edge of the stairwell.

Below she can Sideney working on the door in one curved wall. Banjo is stood over him . . .

> VOICE (O.C.)
>
> (cheerful)
> Hello. What's your name?

Susan turns her head slowly.

It's Teatime.

First she sees the grey, glinting eye. Then the yellow-white one with the tiny dot of a pupil comes into view.

She starts to move her hand but Teatime is there first, dragging the sword scabbard out of her belt.

> TEATIME
> Ah, ah!

He turns and fends her off as she tries to grab it.

> TEATIME
> Well, well, well. White bone handle,
>   rather tasteless skull and bone
>   decoration . . . Death himself's
> second favourite weapon, am I
> right? Oh, my! This must be
> Hogswatch! And this must mean
> that you are Susan, the famous
> granddaughter. Nobility. I'd bow
> . . .

He dances back and forces her into the room with the sword.

INT. TOOTH FAIRY'S CASTLE/TOOTH FAIRY'S ANTE-ROOM – DAY

Susan backs into the room.

TEATIME
. . . but I'm afraid
you'd do something
dreadful.

There is a click, and a little
gasp of excitement from the
wizard working on the door.

MR SIDENEY
Yes! Yes! Left-handed
using a wooden pick!
That's simple!

He sees that even Susan is
looking at him, and coughs
nervously.

MR SIDENEY
Er, I've got the fifth lock
open, Mister Teatime! Not a
problem. They're just based on
Woodeley's occult sequence. Any
fool could do it if they knew
that!

TEATIME
I know it.

Teatime doesn't take his eyes off
Susan.

SUSAN
How do you know who I am?

TEATIME
Oh, easy, Twurp's Peerage.
Family motto: Non temetis messor. Your
father was well
known. Went a
long way very
fast. As for
your grandfather
. . . honestly,
that motto,'Fear
Not the Reaper
. . .' Is that
good taste? Of
course, you
don't need to
fear him, do
you? Or do you?

SUSAN
I don't know what you're
talking about. Who are you,
anyway?

TEATIME
I beg your pardon. My name
is Teh-ah-time-eh, Jonathan
Teh-ah-time-eh. At your
service.

SUSAN
You mean . . . like around
four o'clock in the
afternoon?

TEATIME
No. I did say Teh-ah-time-
eh. Please don't try to
break my concentration by
annoying me. How are you
getting on, Mr Sideney? If it's just
according to Woodeley's sequence,
number 6 should be copper and blue-
green light.

He still doesn't break her gaze.

TEATIME
Do you think your grandfather will try
to rescue you? But now I have his
sword, you see. I wonder . . .

There is the *snickersnicker* sound of scissors from
outside the door. Sideney jumps and fumbles at the
lock.

TEATIME
All fingers and thumbs, Mr Sideney?

There is another click.

MR SIDENEY
Sixth lock, Mister Teatime!

TEATIME
Really. But it may not be all important
now. Thank you, anyway. You've been
most helpful.

MR SIDENEY
Er . . .

TEATIME

    Yes, you may go.

Sideney doesn't even bother to pick up his books and
tools, but runs out of the room as fast as he can.

SUSAN

    Is that all you're here for? A robbery?
    Like a petty thief?

Teatime dances excitedly.

TEATIME

    A thief? Me? I'm not a thief,
    madam.

Medium Dave hurries into the room.

Teatime gestures to Medium Dave.

TEATIME

    No, these gentlemen are thieves.
    Common robbers. Decent types,
    although you wouldn't necessarily
    want to watch them eat, for
    example. That's Medium Dave and
    exhibit B is Banjo. He can talk.

Medium Dave nods at Susan. She sees the
look in his eyes. Maybe there is
something she can use . . .

INT. TOOTH FAIRY'S CASTLE/STAIRS – DAY

Sideney doesn't look back as he scurries
down the stairs and . . . bumps into
Bilious and Violet moving much more
slowly.

MR SIDENEY

    Uh!

He pushes past them.

VIOLET

    Who are you?

MR SIDENEY

    I'm . . . incognito.

Sideney disappears down the stairs in front of them.

                         VIOLET
              Looked like a wizard to me.

And then Sideney is suddenly running back up towards
them.

Shaking like a leaf, Bilious stands in front of Violet,
as if to defend her.

Sideney freezes on the spot.

Convinced he's had this heroic effect, Bilious puffs
his chest. He's about to speak when just out of the
corner of his eye he sees something move on the stairs
on the opposite side of the shaft . . . it flashes like
metal blades catching the light.

Sideney gasps and stares at the opposite stairs. His
thumb rises to his mouth as he turns and stares at
Bilious. In the distance we can hear the faint sound of
snipping.

                         VIOLET
                   (innocently)
              Did you suck your thumb when you were
              little?

Sideney pulls his thumb quickly from his mouth.

Bilious looks behind Sideney and points.

                         BILIOUS
                   (really interested)
              It's the Scissor Man . . .

                       MR SIDENEY
              Shutupshutupshutup!

Sideney shuts his eyes.

Violet grabs Bilious and waves frantically towards the
bottom of the stairs.

                       MR SIDENEY
              Kids believe all kinds of crap! But I'm
              grown up now, right, and . . .

Bilious and Violet hurry away.

Sideney's eyes are shut tight. The *snip, snip* sound
snickers again. It sounds very close now. He turns and
stares at the LOOMING SHADOW of something like a lizard

on its hind legs, but almost entirely like
something made out of blades, moving towards
him . . .

The *snickersnicker* of the SCISSOR MAN's
thousand blades is deafening.

INT. TOOTH FAIRY'S CASTLE/TOOTH FAIRY'S ANTE-ROOM - DAY

Teatime stares at Susan and then suddenly is
much closer.

> TEATIME
> No more Hogfather. And that's only
> the start. I'll be able to make
> people believe anything I want.

There is a rumble like an avalanche, a long
way off. The dormant Banjo has awakened.
His enormous hands start to bunch.

> BANJO
> What's dis? You said no more
> Hogfather.

He stands up, like a mountain range.

Teatime stares at him and then glances at Medium Dave.

> TEATIME
> He does know what we've been doing,
> doesn't he? You did tell him?

Medium Dave shrugs.

> BANJO
> Dere's got to be a Hogfather. Dere's
> always a Hogfather.

Susan looks down. Grey blotches are speeding across the
white marble. She is standing in a pool of grey. So is
Banjo. And around Teatime the dots bounce and recoil
like wasps around a pot of jam.

Teatime points at Susan.

> TEATIME
> She did it. She killed him.

The sheer playground effrontery of it shocks Susan.

                    SUSAN
No I didn't. He—

                    TEATIME
Did!

                    SUSAN
Didn't!

                    TEATIME
Did!

Banjo's big bald head turns towards her.

                    BANJO
What's dis about the Hogfather?

                    SUSAN
I don't think he's dead. But Teatime
has made him very ill . . .

                    TEATIME
Who cares? When this is over, Banjo,
you'll have as many presents as you
want. Trust me!

                    BANJO
Dere's got to be a Hogfather. Else
dere's no Hogswatch.

                    TEATIME
It's just another solar festival. It . . .

Medium Dave stands up. He has his hand on his sword.

                    MEDIUM DAVE
Me and Banjo are going. Banjo? You come
with me right now!

Teatime points to Susan.

                    TEATIME
Grab her, Banjo. It's all her fault!

Banjo lumbers a few steps in Susan's direction, and
then stops.

                    BANJO
Our mam said no hittin' girls. No
touchin' 'em. No pullin' 'm hair . . .

Teatime rolls his one good eye.

                    TEATIME
              She's not a girl . . .

He turns to Susan with a vicious smile.

                    TEATIME
              . . . she's a freak.

Susan stares at him.

Around his feet the greyness seems to be boiling in the
stone, following his feet as they move. And it is
around Banjo, too.

                    SUSAN
                (sweetly)
              I think I know you, Teatime. You're the
              mad kid they're all scared of, right?

                    TEATIME
              Banjo? I said grab her . . .

                    BANJO
              Our mam said . . .

                    SUSAN
              The kid who didn't know the difference
              between chucking a stone at a cat and
              setting it on fire.

To her delight he glares at her.

                    TEATIME
              I said shut up! Get her, Banjo!

There is a touch of vibrato in Teatime's
voice that hasn't been there before.

                    SUSAN
              The kind of little boy . . . who
              looks up dolls' dresses . . .

                    TEATIME
              I didn't!

Banjo looks worried.

                    BANJO
              Our mam said . . .

                    TEATIME
              Oh, to blazes with your mam!

There is a whisper of steel as Medium Dave draws his
sword.

                    MEDIUM DAVE
          What'd you say about our mam?

Now Teatime's having to concentrate on three people.

                      SUSAN
          I bet no one wanted to play with you.
          Not the kid with no friends.

                     TEATIME
              (screaming)
          Banjo! You do what I tell you!

The monstrous man is beside her now. His
face is twisted in an agony of indecision.
His enormous fists clench and unclench.

                      BANJO
          Our . . . Our mam . . . Our mam said . . .

The grey marks flow across the floor and
form a pool of shadow which grows darker and
higher with astonishing speed. It towers
over the three men, and grows a shape.

                 MA LILYWHITE (V.O.)
          Have you been a bad boy, Banjo?

The huge woman towers over all three men. In
one meaty hand it is holding a bundle of birch twigs as
thick as a man's arm. The thing growls.

Medium Dave looks up into the enormous face of MA
LILYWHITE. Every pore is a pothole. Every brown tooth
is a tombstone.

                 MA LILYWHITE (V.O.)
          You been letting him get into trouble,
          our Davey? You have, ain't you?

He backs away.

                    MEDIUM DAVE
          No, Mum . . . no, Mum . . .

                 MA LILYWHITE (V.O.)
          You need a good hiding, Banjo? You been
          playing with girls again?

Banjo sags on to his knees, tears of misery rolling
down his face.

                    BANJO
          Sorry Mum sorry sorry Mum noooohhh Mum
          sorry Mum sorry sorry . . .

Then the figure turns to Medium Dave again.

The sword drops out of his hand. His face seems to
melt. Medium Dave starts to cry.

                  MEDIUM DAVE
          No Mum no Mum no Mum nooooh Mum . . .

He gives a gurgle and collapses, clutching his chest.
And vanishes.

Teatime starts to laugh.

Susan taps him on the shoulder and as he looks round,
hits him as hard as she can across the face.

But . . . his hand moves faster and catches her wrist.
It is like striking an iron bar.

                    TEATIME
          Oh, no. I don't think so.

Out of the corner of her eye, Susan sees Banjo crawling
across the floor to where his brother had been. Ma
Lilywhite has vanished.

                    TEATIME
          This place gets into your head, doesn't
          it? It pokes around to find out how to
          deal with you. Well, I'm in touch with
          my inner child.

He reaches out with his other hand and grabs her hair,
pulling her head down.

Susan screams.

                    TEATIME
          (whispering)
          And it's much more fun.

Susan feels his grip lessen. There's a wet thump like a
piece of steak hitting a slab and Teatime goes past
her, on his back.

                              BANJO
              No pullin' girls' hair. That's bad.

Teatime bounces up like an acrobat and steadies himself
on the railing of the stairwell. Then he draws the
sword. The blade is invisible in the bright light of
the tower.

                             TEATIME
              It's true what the stories say, then.
              So thin you can't see it. I'm going to
              have such fun with it.

He waves it at them.

                             TEATIME
              So light.

                              SUSAN
              You wouldn't dare use it. My
              grandfather will come after you.

She walks towards him. She sees one eye twitch.

                             TEATIME
              He comes after everyone. But I'll be
              ready for him.

                              SUSAN
              He's very singleminded.

Susan is much closer now.

                             TEATIME
              Ah, a man after my own heart.

He brings the sword around. She doesn't even have time
to duck. And doesn't even try to when he swings the
sword back again.

                              SUSAN
              It doesn't work here. The blade doesn't
              exist here. There's no Death here!

She slaps him across the face.

                              SUSAN
                (brightly)
              Hi, Inner Child! I'm the Inner
              Babysitter!

She doesn't punch. She just thrusts out an arm, palm

first, catching him under the chin and lifting him
backwards over the rail.

He somersaults . . . and somehow manages with his free
arm to grab at hers.

Susan's feet come off the ground, and she is over the
rail. She catches it with her other hand.

Teatime swings from her arm, staring upwards with a
thoughtful expression.

She sees him grip the sword hilt in his teeth and reach
down to his belt.

Susan kicks down and hits him on the ear.

The cloth of her sleeve begins to tear.

Teatime tries to get another grip.

She kicks again and the dress rips.

For an instant he holds on to nothing and then, still
wearing the expression of someone trying to solve a
complex problem, he falls away, spinning, getting
smaller . . .

INT. TOOTH FAIRY'S CASTLE/FOOT OF TOWER - DAY

Teatime hits the pile of teeth, sending them splashing
across the marble and out of the circle.

There is a flash before the waves of light subside.

Teatime jerks for a moment . . . and vanishes.

INT. UNSEEN UNIVERSITY/GREAT HALL - NIGHT

The Bursar sits nervously amid the cacophony of wizards
in full-on banquet mode. He eyes the nearest roast pig
with nervous anticipation. He tucks his napkin firmly
under his chin and raises a large fork.

There is a sound like coarse fabric ripping, somewhere
in the air in front of the Bursar, and a crash as
something lands on top of the roast pig. Roast potatoes
and gravy fill the air. The apple that had been in the
pig's mouth is violently expelled and hits the Bursar
on the forehead.

He blinks, looks down, and finds he is about to plunge his fork into a human head.

                    BURSAR
          (murmuring)
     Ahaha.

The wizards heave aside the overturned dishes and smashed crockery.

                LECTURER IN RECENT RUNES
     Is he dead?

Ponder puts his ear to the fallen man's chest.

                    PONDER STIBBONS
     He's not breathing!

                CHAIR OF INDEFINITE STUDIES
     Breathing spell, breathing spell. Er
     . . . Spolt's Forthright Respirator,
     perhaps? I think I've got it written
     down somewhere . . .

Ridcully reaches through the wizards and pulls out the black-clad man by a leg. He holds him upside down in his big hand and thumps him heavily on the back.

The corpse makes a noise somewhere between a choke and a cough.

                    RIDCULLY
     Make some space, you fellows!

The Archchancellor clears an area of table with one sweep of his spare arm.

The corpse opens his eyes. It's TEATIME.

He has a very close-up view of Ridcully's nose.

                    PONDER STIBBONS
     Excuse me, excuse me.

Ponder leans over with his notebook open.

                    PONDER STIBBONS
     But this is vitally important for the
     advancement of natural philosophy. Did
     you see any bright lights? Was there a
     shining tunnel? Did . . .

Ridcully pulls him away.

                    RIDCULLY
        What's all this, Mr Stibbons?

                 PONDER STIBBONS
        I really should talk to him, sir. He's
        had a near-death experience!

                    RIDCULLY
        We all have. It's called 'living'. Pour
        the poor lad a glass of spirits and put
        that damn pencil away.

                    TEATIME
        Uh . . . This must be Unseen
        University? And you are all wizards?

                    RIDCULLY
        Now, just you lie still.

But Teatime has already risen on his elbows.

                    TEATIME
        There was a sword.

                    THE DEAN
        Oh, it's fallen on the floor.

The Dean reaches down.

                    THE DEAN
        But it looks as though it's . . .

The wizards look at the large curved slice of
table falling away. Something has cut through
everything: wood, cloth, plates, cutlery,
food.

                    THE DEAN
        Did I do that?

The Dean raises his hand. The other wizards scatter.

                    TEATIME
        Excuse me, sir.

Teatime takes the sword-hilt from him.

                    TEATIME
        I really must be off.

He runs from the hall.

>   LECTURER IN RECENT RUNES
>   He won't get far. The main doors are
>   locked in accordance with
>   Archchancellor Spode's Rules.

>   RIDCULLY
>   Won't get far while holding a sword
>   that appears to be able to cut through
>   anything.

There is the sound of falling wood.

INT. TOOTH FAIRY'S CASTLE/BALCONY BY ANTE-ROOM - NIGHT

A hand like a bunch of bananas pulls Susan
back over the rail.

>   BANJO
>   You can get into trouble, hittin'
>   girls. No playin' with girls.

There is a click behind them.

The doors have swung open. Cold white mist
rolls out across the floor.

>   BANJO
>   Wot am I gonna do now?

She stares at his big, tear-stained face. She
pulls a handkerchief out of her pocket, dabs it
over the worst parts and then tucks it into his hand.

Susan watches him plod off.

She looks at the white doorway.

INT. TOOTH FAIRY'S CASTLE/WHITE ROOM - DAY

The room beyond the door is entirely white. The mist
that swirls at knee-level deadens even the sound of her
footsteps.

There is just a large four-poster bed, old and dusty,
and lying among the mounds of pillows is a frail OLD
LADY in a mob-cap. The old woman turns her head and
smiles at Susan.

> TOOTH FAIRY
> Hello, my dear.

Susan looks at the picture-perfect patchwork quilt.

> SUSAN
> No.

> TOOTH FAIRY
> Sorry, dear.

> SUSAN
> You're not the Tooth Fairy.

> TOOTH FAIRY
> Oh, I am, dear.

> SUSAN
> Oh, Grandma, what big teeth you have
> . . . Good grief, you've even got a
> shawl, oh dear.

> TOOTH FAIRY
> I don't understand, lovey . . .

> SUSAN
> You forgot the rocking chair. I always
> thought there'd be a rocking chair . . .

Susan moves closer to her.

> SUSAN
> I don't think you're real.
> There's not a little old woman
> in a shawl running this place.
> You're out of my head. That's
> how you defend yourself . . .
> You poke around in people's
> heads and find the things that
> work—

The old woman changes into a jelly-like
blob with a terrible grin.

> SUSAN
> Nope. It's horrible, but it
> doesn't frighten me.

Then she turns into a spider, then a
dog and a rat.

215

SUSAN
I like spiders. Dogs? No. Rats are
fine, I like rats.

A screaming monster face.

SUSAN
Sorry, is anyone frightened of that?

She grabs at the thing and this time the
shape stays. It is a small, wizened monkey,
but with big deep eyes under a brow
overhanging like a balcony. Its hair is
grey and lank. It struggles weakly in her
grasp, and wheezes.

THE BOGEYMAN
I . . . I . . .

The creature hangs limp. She lets it down again.

SUSAN
You're a Bogeyman, aren't you?

It collapses in a heap when she takes her hand away.

THE BOGEYMAN
. . . not a . . . the . . .

SUSAN
The first Bogeyman?

And she sees how rangy it is, how white- and grey-
streaked its hair, how the skin is stretched over the
bones . . .

SUSAN
You look terrible.

THE BOGEYMAN
. . . thank you very much . . .

SUSAN
I mean ill.

Susan sits down on the bed.

The black, sunken eyes glint at her and suddenly the
thing rears up, bony arms waving.

THE BOGEYMAN
I used to jump out on them and say

'boo!'. But then I got to like 'em.
Only children were frightened of me. I
mean, what's to be scared of? Big eyes,
bony arms . . .

He waves them unconvincingly.

> THE BOGEYMAN
> Then I discovered that there were much
> worse things than me and I wanted to
> protect them, keep them safe from the
> really bad things. So I built all this
> to be a safe place.

Susan tries not to shudder.

> SUSAN
> And the teeth?

> THE BOGEYMAN
> Oh, if you leave all those teeth
> around anything could happen . . .

> SUSAN
> Anything nearly did.

The Bogeyman starts to shake.

> SUSAN
> So you are the Tooth Fairy, then?

> THE BOGEYMAN
> Yes, I . . . and then they came
> . . . stealing . . . I'm too weak
> to look after them any more.

The Bogeyman groans.

> THE BOGEYMAN
> . . . you . . . don't die here.
> Just get old, listening to the
> laughter . . .

Susan nods. Faintly we can hear the distant
chatter of children.

The Bogeyman fades.

> SUSAN
> Don't worry about the teeth. I'll
> make them safe again.

INT. TOOTH FAIRY'S CASTLE/FOOT OF TOWER - DAY

Banjo has a BROOM and MOP. The circle is empty and he is carefully washing the chalk away.

Susan comes down the steps and goes over to him.

> SUSAN
I think it would be a good idea if you did the Tooth Fairy's job, Banjo.

> BANJO
Will that be all right, miss? Won't the Tooth Fairy mind?

> SUSAN
You . . . do it until she comes back.

> BANJO
So who's gonna tell me what to do?

> SUSAN
No one's ever going to tell you what to do again, Banjo.

                    BANJO
        Thank you, miss. I will keep the teeth
        safe, miss. Er.

The big pink face looks at her.

                    SUSAN
        Yes, Banjo?

                    BANJO
        Can I have a puppy, miss? I had a
        kitten once, miss, but our mam drownded
        it 'cos it was dirty.

Susan thinks for a moment.

                    SUSAN
        I think it'll turn up quite soon,
        Banjo.

                    BANJO
        Thank you, miss.

Susan looks back up the tower, then turns to leave.
Just as she does Bilious bursts in, followed by Violet.
He is waving a branch like a club. He sees Banjo. He
braces himself, closes his eyes and hurls himself
towards him.

Susan watches as Bilious bounces off the giant figure
and lands flat on his back. He still tries to wave the
branch.

                    BILIOUS
        Violet talked about it and we thought
        we ought to come back and help.

Banjo reaches out a hand and smiles his gappy smile.

Now Bilious is really confused.

                    SUSAN
        It's okay. They're all gone.

Bilious is almost convinced.

                    SUSAN
        And Banjo needed a new job.

Bilious lowers the branch and takes Banjo's hand.

VIOLET

That's funny. So does Bili.

Susan looks at the oh God. He gives her a pleading look.

SUSAN

Look, why don't you two make yourselves useful and help Banjo clear up this mess. He's . . . more or less running the place now.

Violet laughs.

VIOLET

But he's . . .

SUSAN

He's in charge.

Bilious and Violet look into each other's eyes.

VIOLET

We'd . . . love to help Banjo . . . together.

SUSAN

Good. Have fun. Now I'm going home.

And with that she walks towards the door and opens it . . .

SUSAN

This is a hell of a way to spend Hogswatch.

EXT. STREET/ANKH-MORPORK - NIGHT

The Auditors flutter anxiously by the 'soft place' in the wall in the dead-end street.

AUDITOR 3

It's not our fault.

AUDITOR 4

It's Death's fault. He interfered, after all.

AUDITOR 2

Er . . . not exactly.

                    AUDITOR 3
Oh, come on. He got the girl involved.

                    AUDITOR 2
Er . . . no. She got herself involved.

                    AUDITOR 3
Yes, but he told her . . .

                    AUDITOR 2
No. He didn't. In fact he specifically
did not tell . . .

                    AUDITOR 3
Damn!

                    AUDITOR 2
On the other hand . . .

The robes turn towards it.

                    AUDITOR 2
The Assassin did exceed his remit . . .

                    AUDITOR 4
. . . there will be a rebate from the
Guild of Assassins?

                    AUDITOR 3
Irrelevant if blame is inappropriately
levelled.

                    AUDITOR 2
There's no actual evidence. Nothing
written down. Some humans got excited
and decided to attack the Tooth Fairy's
country. This is unfortunate, but
nothing to do with us. We are shocked,
of course.

                    AUDITOR 1
Regrettably, there is evidence.

Now they're starting to panic.

                    AUDITOR 4
There will be an enquiry.

                    AUDITOR 3
Names will be taken.

                         AUDITOR 2
          We don't have names.

                         AUDITOR 1
          We will be given names.

                         AUDITOR 4
          Then they will be taken away.

They pause.

                         AUDITOR 3
          But what about the Hogfather?

                         AUDITOR 1
          Ah. The interminable loose end.

They hover for a while, in unspeaking panic. Eventually
. . .

                         AUDITOR 2
          We may have to take . . . a risk.

                         AUDITOR 4
          Not . . . an actual physical risk?

EXT. GAITER'S HOUSE - NIGHT

Binky walks towards the house.

                         SUSAN
               (to herself)
          Home . . .

Binky stops. She stares at his ears for a moment, and
then urges him forward. He whinnies, and doesn't budge.

A skeletal hand grabs his bridle. DEATH materialises.

                         DEATH
          IT IS NOT OVER.

Susan sags.

                         SUSAN
          What is?

                         SUSAN
          Look, I went . . .

                         DEATH
          YES. I KNOW. THE CONTROL OF BELIEF.

                         SUSAN
          And what were you doing?

          DEATH
          I TOO HAVE
          DONE WHAT I
          SET OUT TO DO.
          I HAVE KEPT A
          SPACE. A
          MILLION
          CARPETS WITH
          SOOTY
          BOOTMARKS,
          MILLIONS OF
          FILLED
          STOCKINGS, ALL
          THOSE ROOFS
          WITH RUNNER
          MARKS ON THEM
          . . .
          DISBELIEF WILL
          FIND IT HARD
          GOING IN THE
          FACE OF THAT.

          SUSAN
          So what have I
          got to do now?

          DEATH
          I WILL STEER.

DEATH climbs into the
saddle and reaches
around her for the reins.

                         DEATH
          YOU MUST BRING THE HOGFATHER HOME.

                         SUSAN
          Oh, and why must I?

                         DEATH
          SO THAT THE SUN WILL RISE.

A skeletal foot kicks against Binky's side and the
horse leaps forward.

EXT. ICY MOUNTAINS – NIGHT

Binky, carrying DEATH and Susan, gallops through the icy mountains.

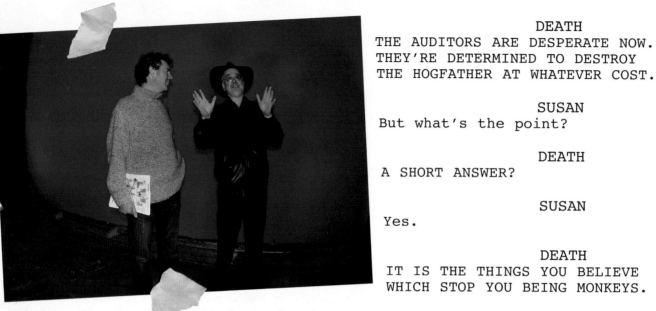

                    DEATH
THE AUDITORS ARE DESPERATE NOW.
THEY'RE DETERMINED TO DESTROY
THE HOGFATHER AT WHATEVER COST.

                    SUSAN
But what's the point?

                    DEATH
A SHORT ANSWER?

                    SUSAN
Yes.

                    DEATH
IT IS THE THINGS YOU BELIEVE
WHICH STOP YOU BEING MONKEYS.

The mists part. Sharp peaks are around them, lit by the glow off the snow.

               SUSAN
     These look like the mountains where the
     Castle of Bones was.

               DEATH
     THEY ARE.

Binky canters low over the snow.

Susan stares down out of sheer annoyance, and sees something below.

Small dark shapes move across the whiteness, running as if they are in pursuit of something: hunters . . . And then . . . she sees movement in the snow, a blurred, dark shape dodging and skidding and never clear: the hunted.

Binky drops until his hooves graze the tops of the pine trees.

Now they are lower she can see the hunters clearly. They are large dogs. Their quarry is indistinct, dodging among snowdrifts, keeping to the cover of snow-laden bushes.

A drift explodes. Something big and long and blue-black
rises through the flying snow like a sounding whale.

                    SUSAN
        It's a pig!

                    DEATH
        A BOAR.

She can hear the panting of the creature. The
dogs make no sound at all. Blood streams onto
the snow from the wounds they have already
managed to inflict.

                    SUSAN
        This . . . boar is the . . .

                    DEATH
        YES. THE HOGFATHER AS HE BEGAN.

                    SUSAN
        And they want to kill him . . .

                    DEATH
        NO, NOT JUST KILL HIM IN THIS SHAPE.
        THEY WANT TO TAKE AWAY HIS REAL LIFE,
        TAKE AWAY HIS SOUL, TAKE AWAY
        EVERYTHING.

DEATH points towards the precipice.

                    DEATH
        THEY DRIVE IT TOWARDS THE CLIFF.
        THEY'VE GONE QUITE MAD.THEY MUST NOT
        BE ALLOWED TO BRING HIM DOWN.

                    SUSAN
        Well, stop them!

                    DEATH
        THIS IS A HUMAN THING.

DEATH nods his head towards the
boar.

Binky is keeping level with it now,
barely a few feet away.

Realisation dawns on Susan's face.
She glances ahead. The snowfield
has a cut-off look.

                              DEATH
           YOU MUST.

     CAMERA on Susan's face. DEATH's voice is in her head.

                           DEATH (V.O.)
           WHEN HE REACHES THE EDGE, THERE HE WILL
           STAND AT BAY. HE MUST NOT. UNDERSTAND?
           THESE ARE NOT REAL DOGS. IF THEY CATCH
           HIM, HE WON'T JUST DIE, HE WILL . . .
           NEVER BE . . .

Susan leaps. For a moment she floats through the air,
dress streaming behind her, arms outstretched . . .

And she lands on the animal's back. It stumbles for a
moment and then rights itself. Susan's arms cling to
its neck and her face is buried in its sharp bristles.
She scrunches up her nose from the stink of sweat, and
blood, and pig.

And suddenly there is a lack of landscape in front of
her.

The boar ploughs into the snow on the edge of the drop,
almost flinging her off, and turns to face the hounds.

There are four of them. And not the big floppy sort.

She rams her heels in and grabs a pig's ear in each
hand. She hauls them hard to one side.

                              SUSAN
           Turn left!

To her amazement the boar grunts, prances on the lip of
the precipice and scrambles away.

The hounds flounder as they turn to follow skittering
feet along the edge of the plateau with its cavernous
drop.

The dogs are flying at the boar's heels again.

Susan looks around in the grey, sightless air for
somewhere, some way . . .

EXT. NARROW RIDGE - NIGHT

. . . and there is.

Ahead there is a shoulder of rock, a giant knife-edge connecting this plain to the hills beyond like a narrow foot-bridge. It is sharp, a thin line of snow with chilly depths on either side.

The boar reaches the edge and hesitates. Susan puts her head down and digs her heels in again.

Then, snout down, legs moving like pistons, the beast plunges out onto the rock ridge. Snow sprays up as its trotters seek for purchase.

                    SUSAN
          That's right, that's right, that . . .

A trotter slips.

The other feet scrabble at icy rock.

Susan flings herself the other way, clinging to the neck, and looks down to the dragging abyss under her feet.

There is nothing there.

Powdered ice makes her eyes sting. A flailing trotter almost slams against her head.

The creature's eye is inches away. It is as if someone is looking back at her . . .

A foot catches the rock.

Susan kicks herself upwards in one last effort.

Boar and woman rock for a moment and then a trotter catches a footing and the boar plunges forward along the ridge.

Susan risks a look behind.

The dogs are fast approaching the rock ridge.

Then suddenly another shock underfoot. Snow flies up.

Her world tilts . . .

The boar's muscles bunch as it leaps.

As its back legs leave the ground, a slab of ice and rock comes away and begins the long slide into darkness.

The creature lands. Susan is thrown off and tumbles into deep snow. She flails around madly.

Her hand finds a snow-encrusted branch.

A few feet away the boar lies on its side, steaming and panting.

She pulls herself upright.

The spur here widens out into a hill, with a few frosted trees on it.

The dogs have reached the gap on the other side and are milling round, struggling to prevent themselves slipping.

She puts both hands around the branch and heaves; it comes away with a crack, and she waves it like a club.

                    SUSAN
Come on. Jump! Just you
try it! Come on!

One does.

Susan spins and brings the branch round on the upswing, lifting the animal off its feet and out over the edge.

For a moment the shape wavers and then, howling, it drops out of sight.

She dances a few steps of rage and triumph.

                    SUSAN
          Yes! Yes! Who wants some? Anyone else?

The other dogs look her in the eye. They don't want any.

Finally, after one or two nervous attempts, they turn, still sliding, and try to make it back to the plateau.

A FIGURE bars their way.

It seems to be made of snow, three balls of snow piled on one another. It has black dots for eyes. A semi-circle of more dots form the semblance of a mouth. There is a carrot for the nose.

And, for the arms, there appear to be two twigs . . . at this distance, anyway. One of the twigs is holding a long curved stick . . . A SCYTHE, in fact.

The dogs back away.

The snow breaks off the snowman in chunks, revealing a gaunt figure in a flapping black robe.

DEATH spits out the carrot.

                    DEATH
          HO. HO. HO.

The grey bodies smear and ripple as the hounds try desperately to change their shape.

                    DEATH
          YOU COULDN'T RESIST IT IN THE END? A
          MISTAKE, I FANCY.

He touches the scythe. There is a click as the blade flashes into life.

                    DEATH
          IT GETS UNDER YOUR
          SKIN, LIFE.

DEATH steps forward.

                    DEATH
          SPEAKING
          METAPHORICALLY, OF
          COURSE. IT'S A HABIT
          THAT'S HARD TO GIVE UP.
          ONE PUFF OF BREATH IS
          NEVER ENOUGH. YOU'LL
          FIND YOU WANT TO TAKE
          ANOTHER.

A dog starts to slip on the
snow and scrabbles desperately
to save itself from the long,
cold drop.

                              DEATH
          AND, YOU SEE, THE MORE YOU STRUGGLE FOR
          EVERY MOMENT, THE MORE ALIVE YOU STAY
          . . . WHICH IS WHERE I COME IN, AS A
          MATTER OF FACT.

The leading dog manages, for a moment, to become a grey
figure and manages to speak.

                              AUDITOR 2
          You cannot do this; there are rules!

                              DEATH
          YES. THERE ARE RULES. BUT YOU BROKE
          THEM. HOW DARE YOU? HOW DARE YOU?

The scythe blade is a thin blue outline in the grey
light.

DEATH raises a thin finger to where his lips might have
been and suddenly looks thoughtful.

                              DEATH
          AND NOW THERE REMAINS ONLY ONE FINAL
          QUESTION.

He raises his hands. Light flares in his eye-sockets.
As he speaks, avalanches fall in the mountains.

                                          DEATH
                              HAVE YOU BEEN NAUGHTY
                              . . . OR NICE?

                              There is a deathly pause.

                                          DEATH
                              HO. HO. HO.

                              Susan hears the wails die
                              away.

                              The boar lies in white snow
                              that is now red with blood.
                              She kneels down and tries to
                              lift its head.

                              It is dead. One eye stares at
                              nothing. The tongue lolls.

                              Sobs well up inside her and
                              then she drums on its flank
                              with both fists.

                              232

> SUSAN
> No, you can't! We
> saved you! Dying isn't
> how it's supposed to
> go!

A breeze blows up.

Something stirs in the
landscape, something under the
snow. Tree branches shake
gently, dislodging tiny needles
of ice.

The SUN rises.

The light streams over Susan
like a silent gale. It is
dazzling. She crouches back,
raising her forearm to cover
her eyes. The great red ball
turns frost to fire along the
winter branches.

There is a groan.

A MAN lies in the snow where the
boar had been. He is naked
except for an animal skin
loincloth and he is bleeding
everywhere the hounds have
caught him. He is tattooed.
Blue whorls and spirals haunt
his skin, under the blood. He
opens his eyes and stares at
the sky.

Cold light slams into the
mountain peaks, making every
one a blinding, silent
volcano. It rolls onwards,
gushing into the valleys and
thundering up the slopes,
unstoppable . . .

The man heaves himself
unsteadily to his feet, then
slowly raises his arms and,
silhouetted, greets the
RISING SUN.

EXT. MOUNTAIN WOODS - DAWN

Susan follows him as he lurches down through the freezing woods, the snow glowing orange in the risen sun.

The TATTOOED MAN makes a gurgling sound. He lands on his knees in the snow, clutching at his throat and choking. His breath sounds like a saw.

> SUSAN
> What's the matter? What's the matter?

A bird trills, high on a branch. She looks up.

A wren bobs at her and flutters to another twig.

She looks back.

Clothes are appearing on the man now. He is dressed as a DRUID and carrying a golden sickle.

Something hurries through the wood, barely visible except by its shadow. For a moment she glimpses a white hare before it springs away on a new path.

She looks back once more.

Now the man looks older, although he has the same eyes. Thick white robes appear so that he looks very much like a BISHOP with a MITRE. He has the demeanour of a saint.

A bird calls again. This time she doesn't look away. Somehow all the images of him are there at once, and many others too.

EXT. FOREST EDGE - DAWN

Four huge boars stand and steam, in front of the Hogfather's sleigh.

The Hogfather approaches. He seems almost to put on weight in the last few yards. He climbs aboard and sits down. It is almost impossible to see anything other than the huge, red-robed man, ice crystals settling here and there on the cloth. Only in the occasional sparkle of frost is there a hint of hair or tusk.

He shifts on the seat and then reaches down to extricate a false beard, which he holds up questioningly.

                  DEATH (O.S.)
    SORRY.

The voice is behind Susan.

The Hogfather nods at DEATH and then at Susan. Is it thanks?

Then he shakes the reins and clicks his teeth and the sleigh slides away.

DEATH and Susan watch it go.

Now the Hogfather is a red dot on the other side of the valley.

                  SUSAN
    Well, that about wraps it up for this
    dress. I'd just like to ask, purely out
    of academic interest . . . you were
    sure I was going to survive, were you?

                  DEATH
    I WAS QUITE CONFIDENT.

                  SUSAN
    Oh, good.

There is a pause in the conversation.

                  SUSAN
    Now . . . tell me . . .

            DEATH
    WHAT WOULD HAVE HAPPENED
    IF YOU HADN'T SAVED HIM?

            SUSAN
    Yes!

            DEATH
    THE SUN WOULD NOT HAVE RISEN.

            SUSAN
    Really? Then what would have happened,
    pray?

DEATH
A MERE BALL OF FLAMING
GAS WOULD HAVE
ILLUMINATED THE WORLD.

They walk in silence for a
moment.

SUSAN
All right, I'm not
stupid. You're saying
humans need . . .
fantasies to make
life bearable.

DEATH
NO. HUMANS NEED
FANTASY TO BE HUMAN.
TO BE THE PLACE WHERE THE FALLING ANGEL
MEETS THE RISING APE.

SUSAN
With Tooth Fairies? Hogfathers?

DEATH
YES. AS PRACTISE. YOU HAVE TO START OUT
LEARNING TO BELIEVE THE LITTLE LIES.

SUSAN
So we can believe the big ones?

DEATH
YES. JUSTICE. MERCY. DUTY. THAT SORT OF
THING.

SUSAN
They're not the same at all!

DEATH
YOU THINK SO? THEN TAKE THE UNIVERSE
AND GRIND IT DOWN TO THE FINEST POWDER
AND SIEVE IT THROUGH THE FINEST SIEVE
AND THEN SHOW ME ONE ATOM OF JUSTICE,
ONE MOLECULE OF MERCY. AND YET . . .

DEATH waves a hand.

DEATH
. . . YOU TRY TO ACT AS IF THERE IS
SOME IDEAL ORDER IN THE WORLD, AS IF
THERE IS SOME . . . SOME RIGHTNESS IN
THE UNIVERSE BY WHICH IT MAY BE JUDGED.

238

SUSAN
Yes, but people have got to believe
that, or what's the point . . . ?

DEATH
YOU NEED TO BELIEVE IN THINGS THAT
AREN'T TRUE. HOW ELSE CAN THEY BECOME?

EXT. GAITER'S HOUSE – DAY

Binky trots to a standstill outside the house. Susan
climbs down onto the fresh snow. As her boot lands it
MORPHS back into her Governess shoes.

Her hair and clothes are all back to normal
as she stands uncertainly for a moment.

DEATH
(hopeful)
WOULD YOU LIKE TO VISIT FOR HOGSWATCH
DINNER? ALBERT IS FRYING A PUDDING.

SUSAN
I . . . er . . . they're really
expecting me here.

DEATH nods in an understanding way.

SUSAN
Er . . . would you like a drink
before you go?

DEATH
A CUP OF COCOA WOULD BE APPROPRIATE
IN THE CIRCUMSTANCES.

INT. GAITER'S HOUSE/NURSERY – DAY

Susan takes her coat off.

SUSAN
Right. There's biscuits in the tin on
the mantelpiece.

Susan heads with relief into the tiny kitchen.

DEATH sits down in the creaking wicker chair, buries
his feet in the rug and looks around with interest. He
hears the clatter of cups, and then a sound like
indrawn breath, and then silence.

DEATH helps himself to a biscuit from the tin. There are two full stockings hanging from the mantelpiece. He prods them with professional satisfaction. He picks up a HOGSWATCH CARD. It is fully back to normal. The HOGFATHER is the Hogfather once more.

His gaze travels to the door. Susan's Governess coat and hat are hanging on it.

The door opens.

To his horror, DEATH sees a small CHILD of unidentifiable sex come out of the bedroom, amble sleepily across the floor and unhook the stockings from the mantelpiece. It is halfway back before it notices him and then it simply stops and regards him thoughtfully.

                    TWYLA
     Susan's gotta poker, you know.

                    DEATH
     WELL, WELL. INDEED. MY GOODNESS ME.

                    TWYLA
     I fort - thought — all of you knew
     that now. Larst - last — week she
     picked a Bogey up by its nose.

DEATH is for once speechless.

                    TWYLA
     I'll give Gawain his stocking and then
     I'll come an' watch.

The child pads out. DEATH looks to the kitchen.

                    DEATH
     ER . . . SUSAN?

Susan backs out of the kitchen, a kettle in her hand.

There is a figure behind her. In the half-light the sword gleams blue along its blade.

Its glitter reflects off one glass eye.

                    TEATIME
     Well, well, now this is unexpected. A
     family affair?

240

The sword hums back and forth.

>   TEATIME
>   I wonder? Is it possible to kill Death?
>   This must be a very special sword, and
>   it certainly works here . . .

He raises a hand to his mouth for a moment and gives a
little chuckle.

>   TEATIME
>   And of course it might well not be
>   regarded as murder. Possibly it is a
>   civic act. It would be, as they say,
>   The Big One. Stand up, sir. You may
>   have some personal knowledge about your
>   vulnerability, but I'm pretty certain
>   that Susan here would quite definitely
>   die, so I'd rather you didn't try any
>   last-minute stuff.

>   DEATH
>   I AM LAST-MINUTE STUFF.

DEATH stands up.

Teatime circles around carefully, the sword's
tip making little curves in the air.

From the next room comes the sound of someone
trying to blow a whistle quietly.

Susan glances at her grandfather.

>   SUSAN
>   I don't remember them asking for
>   anything that made a noise.

>   DEATH
>   OH, THERE HAS TO BE SOMETHING IN THE
>   STOCKING THAT MAKES A NOISE. OTHERWISE
>   WHAT IS 4.30 A.M. FOR?

>   TEATIME
>   There are children? Oh yes, of course.
>   Call them.

>   SUSAN
>   Certainly not!

>   TEATIME
>   It will be instructive. Educational.

And when your adversary is Death, you
cannot help but be the good guy.

He points the sword at Susan.

                    TEATIME
          I said call them.

Susan glances hopefully at her grandfather.

He nods. For a moment a glow in one eye-
socket flickers off and on, DEATH's
equivalent of a wink.

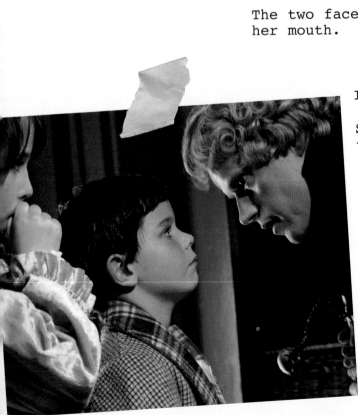

                    SUSAN
          Gawain? Twyla?

The muffled noises stop in the next room.
There is a padding of feet and two solemn
faces appear round the door.

                    TEATIME
               (genially)
          Ah, come in, come in, curly-haired
          tots.

Gawain gives him a steely stare.

                    TEATIME
          I've caught this Bogeyman. What shall
          we do with him, eh?

The two faces turn to DEATH. Twyla puts her thumb in
her mouth.

                    GAWAIN
               (critically)
          It's only a skeleton.

Susan opens her mouth, and the sword swings
towards her. She shuts it again.

                    TEATIME
          Yes, a nasty, creepy, horrible
          skeleton. Scary, eh?

There is a very faint 'pop' as Twyla takes
her thumb out of her mouth.

                    TWYLA
          He's eating a bittit.

SUSAN
        Biscuit.

Susan starts to swing the kettle
in an absentminded way.

                TEATIME
        A creepy bony man in a
        black robe!

He spins round to face Susan.

                TEATIME
        You're fidgeting with that
        kettle. So I expect you're
        thinking of doing something
        creative. Put it down, please. Slowly.

Susan kneels down gently and puts the kettle on the
hearth.

                GAWAIN
        Huh, that's not very creepy, it's just
        bones. And anyway, it's just standing
        there. It's not even making woo-woo
        noises. And anyway, you're creepy. Your
        eye's weird.

                TEATIME
        Really? Then let's see how creepy I can
        be.

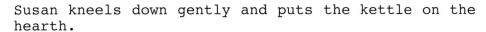

Blue fire crackles along the sword as he raises it.

Susan closes her hand over the poker.

Teatime sees her start to turn. He steps behind DEATH,
sword raised . . .

Susan throws the poker over-arm. It makes a ripping
noise as it shoots through the air, and trails sparks.

It hits DEATH's robe and vanishes. He blinks.

Teatime smiles at Susan. He turns and peers dreamily at
the sword in his hand.

It falls out of his fingers.

DEATH turns and catches it by the handle as it tumbles,
and turns its fall into an upward curve.

Teatime looks down at the poker in his chest as he folds up.

                    TEATIME
          Oh, no. It couldn't have gone through
          you. There are so many ribs and things!

There is another 'pop' as Twyla extracts her thumb.

                    TWYLA
          It only kills monsters.

                    SUSAN
          Stop time now.

DEATH snaps his fingers. The room takes on the greyish
purple of stationary time. The clock pauses its
ticking.

                    SUSAN
          You winked at me! I thought you had a
          plan!

                    DEATH
          INDEED. OH, YES. I PLANNED TO SEE WHAT
          YOU WOULD DO.

                    SUSAN
          Just that?

                    DEATH
          YOU ARE VERY RESOURCEFUL. AND OF COURSE
          YOU HAVE HAD AN EDUCATION.

                    SUSAN
          What?

                    DEATH
          I DID ADD THE SPARKLY STARS AND THE
          NOISE, THOUGH. I THOUGHT THEY WOULD BE
          APPROPRIATE.

                    SUSAN
          And if I hadn't done anything?

                    DEATH
          I DARESAY I WOULD HAVE THOUGHT OF
          SOMETHING. AT THE LAST MINUTE.

                    SUSAN
          That was the last minute!

DEATH

THERE IS ALWAYS TIME FOR ANOTHER LAST
MINUTE.

DEATH prods the fallen Teatime with his foot.

DEATH

STOP PLAYING DEAD, MISTER TEH-AH-TIME-
EH.

The ghost of the Assassin springs up like a Jack-
in-the box, all slightly crazed smiles.

TEATIME

You got it right!

DEATH

OF COURSE.

Teatime begins to fade.

DEATH

I'LL TAKE THE BODY. THAT WILL PREVENT
INCONVENIENT QUESTIONS.

DEATH picks up the corpse and slings it over his
shoulder. There is a sound of something bouncing on
the hearth. He turns and hesitates.

DEATH

ER . . . YOU DID KNOW THE POKER WOULD
GO THROUGH ME?

Susan hesitates, and then smiles.

SUSAN

I was quite confident.

DEATH

AH.

Her grandfather stares at her for a moment and then
turns towards the balcony. And then he seems to
remember something else. He fumbles inside his robe.

DEATH

I HAVE MADE THIS FOR YOU.

She reaches out and takes a square of damp
cardboard. Water drips off the bottom. Somewhere in
the middle, a few brown feathers seemed to have
been glued on.

245

SUSAN
Thank you. Er . . . what is it?

DEATH
ALBERT SAID THERE OUGHT TO BE
SNOW ON IT, BUT IT APPEARS TO
HAVE MELTED. IT IS, OF COURSE, A
HOGSWATCH CARD.

SUSAN
Oh . . .

DEATH
THERE SHOULD HAVE BEEN A ROBIN ON
IT AS WELL, BUT I HAD
CONSIDERABLE DIFFICULTY IN
GETTING IT TO STAY ON.

SUSAN
Ah . . .

DEATH
IT WAS NOT AT ALL CO-OPERATIVE.

SUSAN
Really . . . ?

DEATH
IT DID NOT SEEM TO GET INTO THE
HOGSWATCH SPIRIT AT ALL.

SUSAN
Oh. Good.

She pauses for thought.

SUSAN
Granddad?

DEATH
YES?

SUSAN
Why? I mean, why did you do all this?

He stands quite still for a moment.

DEATH
HUMAN BEINGS MAKE LIFE SO INTERESTING.
DO YOU KNOW THAT IN A UNIVERSE SO FULL
OF WONDERS THEY HAVE MANAGED TO INVENT
BOREDOM? QUITE ASTONISHING.

246

                    SUSAN
    Oh.

                    DEATH
    WELL THEN . . . HAPPY HOGSWATCH.

                    SUSAN
    Yes. Happy Hogswatch.

DEATH pauses again, at the window.

                    DEATH
        AND GOOD NIGHT, CHILDREN . . .
        EVERYWHERE.

EXT. GAITER'S HOUSE/NURSERY - DAY

The CAMERA pulls back from DEATH looking out of the
window and up and away from the snow-covered house . . .

INT. ARCHCHANCELLOR'S BATHROOM - DAY

Warm water cascades off Mustrum Ridcully's pointy
bathing cap.

                    RIDCULLY
        (singing)
        . . . running of the deer,

Ridcully pulls a little brass lever he hasn't seen,
marked ORGAN INTERLOCK.

INT. UNSEEN UNIVERSITY/CHAPEL - DAY

Organ pipes hum with pent-up energy.

A set of knuckles crack. Then the VERY HAIRY HAND OF AN
ORANG-UTAN pulls a handle reading: PRESSURE RELEASE
VALVE.

Just beneath it we see the corner of a little brass
plate with the words: **A Bloody Stupid Johnson Patented**
. . . as the hum of the pipes becomes an urgent
thrumming.

INT. UNSEEN UNIVERSITY/ARCHANCELLOR'S BATHROOM - DAY

Ridcully lathers himself and sings.

> RIDCULLY
> . . . the playing of . . . huh?
> What . . .

There's a thud, a distant gurgling which grows in
volume and the sound of a man under attack from water
in all directions.

EXT. UNSEEN UNIVERSITY/ARCHCHANCELLOR'S BATHROOM - DAY

Later . . . The bathroom is nailed up again and a
notice has been placed on the door, on which is
written:

NOT TO BE USED IN ANY CIRCUMSTANCES. THIS IS IMPORTANT.

INT. ASSASSIN'S GUILD/DOWNEY'S OFFICE - NIGHT

LORD DOWNEY gets up from his desk. A
posse of other ASSASSINS are gathered.
They follow him as he walks down his
office.

> LORD DOWNEY
> It would be . . . inelegant if
> the word 'Teatime' were ever
> mentioned again within the
> guild halls . . . unless it
> is in fact . . . four o'clock
> in the afternoon with
> crumpets.

INT. DEATH'S HOUSE - NIGHT

Albert is frying a pudding on a
stove. He has a roll-up in his mouth.
He magics a flame on the end of his
finger and FINALLY lights the
cigarette. He takes one puff, coughs,
and with a look of disgust throws it away.

248

INT. TOYMAKER'S SHOP - DAY

A long, long time ago . . . the shop door opens.
The little TOYMAKER stops dead.

> DEATH
> YOU HAVE A BIG WOODEN ROCKING HORSE IN
> THE WINDOW.

> TOYMAKER
> Ah, yes, yes, yes. But I'm afraid
> that's a special order for Lord . . .

> DEATH
> HOW MUCH WOULD THIS LORDSHIP HAVE PAID
> YOU?

> TOYMAKER
> Er, we'd agreed twelve dollars but . . .

> DEATH
> I WILL GIVE YOU FIFTY.

> TOYMAKER
> Shall I wrap it up for you?

> DEATH
> NO. I WILL TAKE IT AS IT IS. THANK YOU

DEATH drops a small clinking bag on the counter and
lifts the horse easily.

> DEATH
> INCIDENTALLY, THERE IS A SMALL BOY OUT
> THERE WITH HIS NOSE FROZEN TO THE
> WINDOW. SOME WARM WATER SHOULD DO THE
> TRICK.

And with that, DEATH leaves . . .

INT. DEATH'S HOUSE/SECRET LIFETIMERS ROOM

The Hogfather's Lifetimer is
back on its shelf.

In one piece.

THE END

AFTERWORD

Bringing Discworld to life on the screen in the form of a live-action film for the very first time has been the most challenging and rewarding creative experiences of our lives. The enormity of what we were attempting really struck home from the very first moment that Terry allowed us the rights to adapt *Hogfather*, and again when we got the money in place from Sky and RHI to go ahead with filming. There are an enormous number of people we need to thank, for their help producing this landmark television film, most especially Terry himself, for being so supportive throughout the entire process, from writing to filming, and beyond.

Particular thanks go to the 'A list' creative and production team, not to mention the stellar cast who came to work with us at The Mob, all of whom put in long and arduous hours, well above the call of duty. Every single one of them strove to make their contribution the very best that it could possibly be, and it shows. We owe a huge debt of gratitude to all at BSkyB, James Murdoch, Dawn Airey, James Baker, Ian Lewis, Elaine Pyke et al, who had belief in the project to initially fund the developement process and to support us into production. Thanks also to Richard Woolfe and Hannah Barnes for continuing to support the Franchise on Sky One. We also need to thank Robert Halmi Senior, James Denton and the RHI team in London and New York, our superb international partners.

And now on to the 'makers' of our film. There isn't space to thank everybody by name, but particular thanks must go to Vadim, for although he is a *Mobster* himself, and his vision, energy and enthusiasm usually know no bounds, he was put to the sternest test with us creating this film, and he came through with flying colours, doing a truly awesome job on all levels.

And special thanks also to Gavin Finney B.Sc. and his camera team who gave, through his inspired lighting, such a wonderfully Discworldy feel to the film; to Ricky Eyres for his brilliant set design, and to his props and construction team, who made — with far more creativity than money — some of the most wonderful and awe-inspiring sets and models ever seen on television (and on what was indeed a modest budget by Hollywood standards!). Jane Spicer and her team created wonderful costumes which really captured the mood, and Ros Peat's make-up design was as excellent as we've ever seen. Joe McNally's editing was truly inspired. The fact that they all *got* Discworld — even if they were new to Terry Pratchett's phenomenal world to start with — is what makes *Hogfather* so special.

While we're on the Big Thanks, we must mention Sean Glynn, our Line Producer, who created a fantastic spirit in the camp, and was a great wing man for us, despite the very tough schedule (and thanks for that to Pete Freeman, our dynamic first AD).

Heartfelt gratitude to Mark Benson and The Moving Picture Company, who have supported the project from concept forwards; they have invested a huge amount of time and resources into getting the project off the ground, and the special effects and creatures they designed for the film are truly wonderful.

Finally, we would be churlish indeed if we did not say hearty thanks to our families, who really haven't seen too much of us for the last two years; Kate and Pauline: all your patience and love have kept us going over the long production period.

We do so hope that you enjoy watching *Hogfather*, and we really look forward to turning more of the brilliant Discworld novels into movies in the future.

Rod Brown and Ian Sharples
Producers of Hogfather

P.S. Thanks also to Jo Fletcher of Victor Gollancz, for having the great idea of putting this book together, and for all the time and effort she and Nick May put into making it look so great!

THE CAST

MICHELLE DOCKERY	SUSAN
MARNIX VAN DEN BROEKE	DEATH
MARC WARREN	TEATIME
PETER GUINNESS	MEDIUM DAVE
STEPHEN MARCUS	BANJO
CRAIG CONWAY	CHICKENWIRE
NIGEL PLANER	MR SIDENEY
GEOFFREY HUTCHINS	MR BROWN
TERRY PRATCHETT	THE TOYMAKER
SIR DAVID JASON	ALBERT
JOSS ACKLAND	MUSTRUM RIDCULLY
ED COLEMAN	PONDER STIBBONS
JOHN FRANKLYN-ROBBINS	THE DEAN
ROGER FROST	THE BURSAR
TIMOTHY BATESON	LECTURER IN RECENT RUNES
JOHN BOSWALL	CHAIR OF INDEFINITE STUDIES
JAMES MELLOR	STUDENT WIZARD
TREVOR JONES	MODO
RHODRI MEILIR	BILIOUS
SINEAD MATTHEWS	VIOLET
DAVID WARNER	LORD DOWNEY
NICOLAS TENNANT	CORPORAL NOBBS
RICHARD KATZ	CONSTABLE VISIT
TONY ROBINSON	VERNON CRUMLEY
MARTHA KATZ	BOBBLE HAT CHILD
RACHEL EDWARDS	BOBBLE HAT CHILD'S MOTHER
DOMINIC BORELLI	GROTTO HOGFATHER
AARON BARKER	SMALL BOY
LYDIA ALTMAN	SMALL BOY'S SISTER
ROBERT PORTAL	MR GAITER
DEBORAH WINCKLES	MRS GAITER
MADELENE RAKIC-PLATT	TWYLA
HUGO ALTMAN	GAWAIN
JON RIDGEON	GUEST 1
SHEND	HOGFATHER
ARTHUR WHITE	ERNIE
FOX JACKSON-KEEN	YOUNG ALBERT
DON WETHERHEAD	SLIMAZEL THE BOGEYMAN
JOHN CARTIER	CARTER
JOHNNY WARMAN	TOOTHGUARD 1
TIM PLESTER	TOOTHGUARD 7
BRIDGET TURNER	TOOTHFAIRY / BOGEYMAN
GREGOR HENDERSON-BEGG	PIXIE HELPER
PETER HOLDWAY	AUDITOR 1
ANDRE LAMOTTE	AUDITOR 2
ADAM MARVEL	AUDITOR 3
ANDREW SWAIN	AUDITOR 4
DANNY DACOSTA	VERRUCA GNOME
KEN CAMPBELL	HAIR LOSS FAIRY
MAGGIE McCARTHY	MA LILLYWHITE
NEIL PEARSON	RAVEN

and IAN RICHARDSON as the VOICE OF DEATH